Failure Before Success

Failure Before Success

Teachers Describe What They Learned from Mistakes

Edited by
Julie Warner

ROWMAN & LITTLEFIELD
Lanham • Boulder • New York • London

Published by Rowman & Littlefield
An imprint of The Rowman & Littlefield Publishing Group, Inc.
4501 Forbes Boulevard, Suite 200, Lanham, Maryland 20706
www.rowman.com

6 Tinworth Street, London SE11 5AL, United Kingdom

British Library Cataloguing in Publication Information Available

Library of Congress Cataloging-in-Publication Data on File

ISBN 978-1-4758-5747-4 (cloth : alk. Paper)
ISBN 978-1-4758-5748-1 (pbk. : alk. Paper)
ISBN 978-1-4758-5749-8 (electronic)

∞™ The paper used in this publication meets the minimum requirements of American
National Standard for Information Sciences—Permanence of Paper for Printed Library
Materials, ANSI/NISO Z39.48-1992.

For the teachers who taught through COVID-19.

Contents

Foreword

This welcome book seamlessly, and with engaging honesty, pursues two related themes. The first speaks to how mistakes and failure are inevitable, natural, even necessary, in becoming a seasoned and savvy educator. The contributors' individual stories elucidate the challenges of teaching and how confronting mistakes and failure are part and parcel of dedicated, enlightened, and effective teaching.

The personal experiences shared are also a reminder that seeking error-free or failure-proof practice is not the essence of successful teaching. A teacher who thinks otherwise is likely to be unhappy, unfulfilled, and demoralized—or delusional. Constantly worrying about mistakes and failure and seeking a safe haven insulated from them, or, maybe worse, assuming that perfection is objectively achievable, may actually lead to an unhealthy complacency and stagnation. It may also subvert attention to the larger and inherently messier dimensions of education in the realms of civic, moral, and personal development.

Such tendencies are particularly insidious at the outset of a teaching career when teachers are typically the most insecure and vulnerable, but also when there is the greatest need to learn from missteps. It is not a coincidence that several of the contributors recount mistakes and failures early in their teaching careers. Nor is it a coincidence that they report having sought advice from more experienced colleagues. This book vicariously provides such advice with experienced and thoughtful teachers sharing stories that may edify and inspire those with less experience, while modeling the struggles inherent to teaching.

For both novice or experienced teachers, this collection of chapters counters the notion that perpetually seeking guaranteed or unmitigated success is a formula for good teaching. As is in most fields, such a perspective is inconsistent with the arc of continuous growth and maturity as a practitioner. There can be no innovative, creative, nor contextually adaptive, teaching without some risk of making mistakes and a willingness to tolerate failure, accompanied by a commitment to learn from them in a career-long quest for greater competence.

But, more is needed than an awareness and acceptance of mistakes and failures. As well-illustrated in these chapters, there needs to be analytical reflection about them and systematic attention to mitigating their negative effects. As several of the contributors note, time for such reflection is too often sacrificed to the unrelenting daily demands of teaching, that is, until things go unpleasantly wrong and demand attention. Thus, mistakes and failures are fertile inflexion points for professional insight and growth.

The second, but related, theme is the challenge teachers face in accommodating the multidimensional diversity of their students, which is arguably among the most fundamental challenges of all classroom teaching. How can an appropriate balance be achieved between teaching groups of students while attending to their individual needs? Diversity manifests itself even in classrooms that may on the surface seem homogeneous, with students sharing a common sociocultural background, although such classrooms are becoming increasingly rare in American schools. Differences in ability, personality, motivation, interests, social skills, and so forth can vary considerably in any classroom and always interact with achieving academic goals.

Teachers must look for ways to explicitly accommodate those differences, sometimes overtly (e.g., grouping for instruction) and sometimes less so (e.g., seating arrangements). But, there is also an imperative to take a sincere interest in students' backgrounds and interests beyond their academic acumen. Doing so may be as simple as asking a student who is a baseball fan to explain to classmates how a math lesson on statistics can be applied in that sport. Or, a teacher may give an article about the poetry of rap music to a student who is passionate about that musical form. Several chapters illustrate how such simple, seemingly incidental moves, in classrooms can have cascading positive effects, just as a cutting or insensitive remark can have the opposite effect. Such small things can stick with students for a lifetime.

The challenges of diversity increase exponentially when it includes, as it often does today, sociocultural and linguistic differences. Again, several chapters provide vivid examples. Accommodating such diversity can have practical pedagogical implications such as teaching phonics to students who speak a nonstandard dialect or a language other than English at home.

But, there are also broader implications. Gaining understanding of and acknowledging students' cultural backgrounds can affect motivation and involvement and promote students' sense of personal validation and inclusion. For example, students need both to see themselves in the literary works they read and to vicariously experience a common humanity in characters who live much different lives than their own. It also means a heightened awareness of how pedagogical content may interact with students' sensitivities, sometimes including troubling circumstances and traumatic experiences. Several chapters also address the implications of teachers being outsiders to the communities in which they teach—a situation that amplifies the challenge of dealing with diversity, as well as the need for serious reflection about unfounded assumptions and personal biases.

Those chapters, in particular, invoked a personal experience that took place 50 years ago. As a white, middle-class preservice teacher with a social consciousness, I requested a student teaching assignment at an elementary school in inner-city Chicago. My fifth-grade students were all African American. Before the end of my first day, I realized how far out of my element I was personally, culturally, and professionally, well beyond the normal pedagogical clumsiness of a student-teacher. A string of debilitating (at least to my ego) failures during my first few days led me to try something different.

To satisfy a student-teaching requirement in social studies, I planned a unit on local community. However, the unit was designed to place me in the role of learner and my students as teachers. I challenged the students to teach me, the outsider, about their community. I asked honest questions for clarification and a few that challenged them to extend their own understanding of the role that local community and culture play in everyone's life.

They responded with great enthusiasm and animation. For example, I asked them about what it meant to talk "jive." A boy and girl volunteered immediately to illustrate. They launched spontaneously into an amazing performance that, if I hadn't known otherwise, would have guessed was scripted. That event opened up discussions on a variety of topics including registers of language and their role in connecting speakers with a community—an advanced topic made accessible to fifth-grade students in this instance,

Nonetheless, the unit wasn't by any means a complete success. It never is. But, I learned how I could do it better next time. And, beyond the inherent richness of this multi-cultural experience, I learned several principles that have stuck with me during my entire career, including in my university teaching. Among other things, I always consider ways students can teach me something, how to use them as resources, and how to give them some measure of responsibility for their own learning.

Several contributors point out that their preservice teacher education programs did not adequately prepare them for mistakes, failure, and dealing with the many realities and contextual complexities of practice. Certainly, such programs cannot be expected to prepare future teachers for every possible context and contingency. But, this book suggests that they might do better, impressing on preservice teachers the inevitability of mistakes and failures and how they might deal with them. They might put more emphasis on the importance of reflection, analysis, strategic adjustments, and ways of coping. The personal anecdotes in this book might open doors to fruitful discussion and activities along those lines.

Refreshingly, this book takes a personal, not technical, approach. There is no armchair academic theorizing, nor long lists of scholarly citations. Each chapter reads like an entry in a teacher's reflective journal. But they are also useful gateways to further reading and exploration facilitated by relevant resources listed at the end of chapters.

This more personal approach may also attract readers who are not teachers. In that regard, this book may be palliative to readers outside of education, including policymakers, who too often suffer from the misconception that teaching is primarily a soulless technical skill judged only by test scores.

Finally, this book stands as testimony to a realization that the rewards of teaching—and there are many—do not come automatically, easily, or without at least occasional turmoil, internal and external. In that sense, it is also a reminder that we, as teachers, are in a service-oriented profession, not one entered into mainly for the sake of our personal gratification, or self-actualization. Those rewards are there, but they are by-products, not objects, of our service. Teaching is hard, sometimes gut-wrenching, work. This book helps remind us of that reality.

David Reinking
University of Georgia

Acknowledgments

I want to first thank the educators in these pages who so generously sought to share with others what most of us try to hide.

Two years ago, I was in the audience at a panel discussion on how the influential women on the stage had progressed in their careers while negotiating the competing requirements of everyday life. A woman on the panel I had idolized (and likely idealized) was asked to name the accomplishment she was most proud of.

She had a PhD, led the advocacy work for a major nonprofit focused on educational equity, was a mom, and had her own small business on the side to boot.

I expected her to mention an influential report she'd authored, or a bill she'd helped see its way to the President's desk. Instead, what she said was, "Getting out of bed every morning. Most days, all of the little things just feel like a great struggle."

To hear this woman—always immaculately dressed, poised, and who had a laundry list of achievements to draw from in answering that question—offer this response was edifying, to put it lightly. As she allowed us in the audience to see beyond her surface presentation, I saw myself and my own struggles and felt encouraged.

Around the same time, a friend of mine who is a painter had set up a social media account where she posted works in progress. With each instance I watched her begin to paint, I would wonder how the amorphous and sometimes even visually displeasing starting places could be transformed into the stunning panoramas she was known for.

But watching her apply layer upon layer of pigment I became privy to her process. Putting a masterpiece on canvas became more accessible to me as I saw indications of clouds or trees become lovely landscapes through criss-cross strokes, blending, and patient, concentrated work.

And I thought, why do we as artists, or writers, or other creative professionals conceal our passages? Finished products, while more agreeable than works in progress or a representation of procedure, disguise failed attempts and processes full of correction after correction.

The import of revealing the draft marred with strikethroughs and notes scribbled in margins, of sharing our errors and mistakes in judgment, of being vulnerable about our alterations and adjustments, was an idea I couldn't turn away from as I began to see what these revelations offered.

And so my deepest gratitude goes to Monica R. Almond and Emy Bradbury Whalen who inspired this book.

The interdependence of one's own life and work is difficult to disentangle, but I learned much from my academic mentors Ming Fang He, Michael Moore, Marjorie Siegel, John Broughton, and Chuck Kinzer. I'm fortunate to be a part of a community of friends and colleagues who challenge and support me and who inform my work and life through everyday interactions that are impossible to enumerate. I thank Kip Glazer and Jamie Lee Robinson who consulted with me on some of the ideas in this book.

I am especially grateful for the support of my partner, Bruce J. Packett, who offers an erudite read on anything I give him and who makes everyday life a dream.

Introduction

As far as I could tell, I had no reason to be there. Gazing down at the purple badge with the gold seal in my palm, still warm from the printer, I felt like I'd somehow fast-forwarded through years and years' worth of interstitial moments.

Just a few years prior, I was teaching high school, but somehow there I was outfitted to begin work as an education policy advisor in the U.S. Senate. Walking away from the ID office, I felt drawn toward a hearing room across the hall. First peeking in to ensure that it was vacant, I crept in silently and closed the hulking door, behind which I was safe. Alone, I could let the tears come.

Memories of my teaching life were persistent company. In that life I had near daily feelings of profound incompetence and spent almost as much energy thinking about how I could *appear* as though I knew what I was doing as I did doing the actual work of teaching.

How in the world did I get here? I thought in that empty hearing room.

I later went on to work on education policy in the White House and, most recently, in the internal think tank at the U.S. Department of Education. What I came to realize working all across the highest levels of the education system is that not knowing what you're doing is kind of the point. It's tautological—confusion *has* to come before learning how to do something and then to effect change.

Whether it's advancing in a career by taking on a new role or perfecting a skill or understanding a new idea, nothing materializes apart from the interim steps to getting there with the requisite mistakes and growth.

The many veteran teachers and education experts who contributed to this book have resumes and LinkedIn pages decorated with illustrious awards, prime teaching positions, sought-after certifications, and other markers of status in the field of education.

Indeed, there's no dedicated space for "worst errors" on a job application, and most of us leave our biggest gaffes out of our professional bios. In life and certainly in our careers, we're taught to put our best foot forward. Most of us shy away from the kind of vulnerability displayed in these pages as a means of self-protection. But the shiny, sanitized version of our work as educators belies what it actually takes to do the work we do in classrooms.

Every last one of us with endurance in this complex and often grueling profession have made mistakes along the way. That's because mistakes and even straight-up failure are absolutely essential to developing expertise. While undeniably some mistakes can have negative consequences, for the most part, people tend to learn the most, develop the most, and grow the most from their mistakes.

As for me, I was the kind of teacher who messed up daily.

I was hired to teach high school English as part of a remedial education program in my first teaching job, but I didn't have much of a clue what that would look like until I walked in the school doors to meet my students. As it turned out, that particular school identified limited English proficient students as remedial rather than, well, limited English proficient. That meant I learned in my first year, in addition to everything else first-year teachers contend with, how to teach English as a Second Language rather than the English Language Arts that I had been formally prepared to teach.

"You're new! It will get better," people told me. But it didn't really get better.

I taught from a rolling cart due to a lack of classroom space and I pushed it around the school like a blinking sign advertising where I stood on the professional totem pole. I never seemed to have the materials (or respect) I needed to teach effectively.

We were in rural Georgia among the peanut and cotton fields and most of my students were the children of migrant workers. That meant that I'd teach them for a short period and then, one day, they'd just stop showing up. I didn't have preparation from my teacher training program around how to best teach and support transient students and so I did a pretty poor job despite my good intentions.

Although I completed a whole course dedicated to it on my academic path to becoming a teacher, my classroom management skills were nonexistent. So I learned the hard way that it's in a teacher's best interest not to engage in a power struggle with a teenager in front of his or her peers because a teenager's need to save face is the most powerful force in the universe.

I had no time management skills (or boundaries) and I took work home regularly and did other work for which I wasn't compensated and that went beyond my contract. As a consequence, I was burning out fast.

My clothes were apparently inappropriate, too, because I got called into the principal's office within the first month so she could address my attire. The other teachers had been talking about it, she said, as my face burned hot with embarrassment. My mother had taken me shopping to upgrade my wardrobe for my first professional position after graduating college and I selected an array of what I felt was staid and conservative clothing.

But I was teaching in an evangelical Christian community, and, regardless of the length of my hemline, I was not conforming to sartorial expectations, which were more Anne of Green Gables than corner office chic. Although I spent most of my free time preparing lessons and researching effective teaching strategies, my professionalism was under attack and my confidence plummeted.

These are facts about my teaching career I've never really highlighted, but they offer a fuller picture of my story than what might be called for in a job interview or a book bio.

Daniel Goleman, the author of the groundbreaking book *Emotional Intelligence*, calls the willingness to look at yourself unflinchingly, examining your strengths but also your weaknesses and blind spots, "telling your whole story." He says it promotes your well-being because you get to come out of hiding. I think, too, that telling your whole story helps others, because it models self-acceptance and promotes connection and authenticity over competition and facade.

What you hold in your hands is the whole story.

By way of this volume, I sought to provide a platform for teachers to tell the whole story and to share their journeys to expert, engaged teaching, paved as these paths were with blind spots, failings, missteps, and foibles. The professionals in these pages bravely examined their *whole story* to show how it was that they took a critical incident and moved from mistake to transformation.

Not only does telling the whole story promote well-being, it is the first step toward alchemizing failure into something useful. Duke University professor Sim Sitkin first put forward the concept of "intelligent failure"—the type of failure that is actually *sought after* because it provides valuable knowledge that can help an industry or an organization advance.

Sitkin says intelligent failure is an absolute necessity in contexts that are unpredictable and new—where cookie-cutter approaches most certainly *won't* lead to success because they don't match the unique context. (Some examples of these contexts are testing customer reception of highly innovative products, research and development, or technology-focused businesses.)

Any teacher can tell you that with each class comprising vastly different individual human beings who, when they come in contact, give rise to a very unique dynamic, there's likely no industry that needs to be more agile, responsive, and welcoming of risk-taking than teaching. It stands to reason then that with teaching, each class being a new frontier, experimentation would be just good professional practice—but we must then accept that with experimentation comes failure.

Mistakes, then, are not something to hide, they're a crucial ingredient for growth and something fertile we can mine for lessons about how to do things better.

THE CULTURE OF PERFECT

In addition to my desire to bring mistakes to light and in doing so provide a blueprint for teachers' processes of reflection, learning, and transformation so that other educators can take up similar approaches to learning from practice, by presenting accounts of mistakes, I want to normalize mistake-making and reframe the way we think about mistakes in the field of education.

As Brene Brown asserts in *The Gifts of Imperfection*, the only way to live wholeheartedly is to let go of perfectionism, worrying about what other people think, self-doubt, comparing yourself to others, "supposed-to," and the need to be cool and in control. For too long, education has moved toward boxed solutions, standardized curriculum, and high-stakes accountability, all of which suggest one "right" way of being for teachers. The imperative has been on control and promoting achievement instead of on being authentic and connecting with students, colleagues, and ourselves.

Several recent studies have examined the effects of this culture on student well-being. High-stakes testing has been shown to have a deleterious effect on student mental health, raising anxiety levels and reducing feelings of efficacy and self-esteem. But what about the effects of our failure-averse culture on *teacher* wellness? Kids get one chance to take the end-of-year exam, and teachers often get that same one chance to prove that their teaching was effective when so many schools are using test scores as a measure of good teaching.

Not only does it have a damaging effect on student and teacher well-being, this high-stakes accountability culture in education is, paradoxically, antithetical to learning. We cannot devalue mistakes and actually learn, if learning necessitates a change or transformation of some sort in our abilities or in what we know. Just as confusion is necessary for gaining new knowledge or clarity, mistakes are a key ingredient in the development of new skills in the art and practice of teaching.

I know what you're thinking. That's all fine and good, but it's not in my best interest to advertise my shortcomings.

Believe me, I get it. There's a lot of pressure on teachers to have all the answers. After all, we write the tests and we assign the grades. We are the experts and authority figures in our classrooms and somewhere along the way this translates into endeavoring for perfection. This is to say nothing of teaching in the era of social media. The teacher Instagram-o-sphere is an intimidating place for a new teacher, with curated images of Pinterest-perfect classrooms and video clips showing that minute fraction of the day where things went right.

THE MYTH OF PERFECT TEACHING

It would benefit us all to concede that perfection itself is a myth. It's simply not achievable—because it's subjective! That is to say, no two people will ever see something the same way or make the same value judgment.

Perhaps teaching is even less prone to fit into the "perfect box" than any other profession's central endeavor. Because classrooms are so nuanced a working environment, made up of twenty to thirty highly complex human beings, successful teaching cannot be reduced to one ideal, copybook approach.

Even if I still haven't convinced you that perfection in teaching is not achievable, at least consider the effects that striving for perfection has on teacher wellness. The more we try to strive for perfection, being that it is a quality that does not exist, the more dissatisfaction and discontent results, leading to stress, anxiety, and depression.

Some people are even driven to destructive behaviors because they can't cope with feeling like a failure all the time as they chase ever-elusive perfection. It is of critical importance then that we examine how realistic or unrealistic our beliefs are and start to chip away at those that don't support our well-being. I am passionate about the stories here because I believe they will help you to recalibrate in this way.

MISTAKES AND SELF-COMPASSION

In looking across the submissions in this volume, the key element that emerges within the experiences of the mistake-making experts that allowed them to examine and transform their mistakes into powerful insights is self-compassion.

According to self-compassion researcher Kristin Neff, perfectionism and self-compassion cannot coexist. Neff defines self-compassion as *showing compassion for one's self in instances of perceived inadequacy or failure.* In order to move from mistake to transformation, the educators in this book had to have self-compassion or they would have been unable to not only face mistakes and blind spots without shrinking away or folding, but they also would have lacked the resilience that self-compassion affords us to move forward and learn from our missteps as imperfect human beings.

Beyond its centrality to examining our lives as professionals honing our teaching craft, self-compassion is important for educators for another reason. Educators are often expected to give their entire selves to the job of teaching, to be caretakers in addition to content experts and pedagogical wizards. Images of teachers in popular culture reinforce this mythical, savior mentality built on self-sacrifice.

In my experiences working and talking with teachers, I have seen time and again how often they put themselves last. There is a great need for those in service-oriented fields to develop self-compassion, and especially for teachers to do so, since they are so often giving to others at the expense of giving to themselves.

Kristin Neff asserts that reading about others' mistakes and flaws can help us all acknowledge the shared nature of our imperfect human condition and help us build self-compassion. The reality is that as humans, we all have certain strengths and certain weaknesses. The shared human condition is that we are all imperfect and that is the way it's supposed to be. Wouldn't the world be a better place for us all if more people would tell the whole story thereby fostering self-compassion in themselves and others?

In turn, teacher self-compassion translates to an emotionally supportive climate for students. Teachers who have compassion for themselves and see what they do as part of a growth trajectory create positive, prosocial, and supportive classroom climates as a result. These kinds of classrooms give rise to increased student motivation, engagement, and a sense of belonging.

IN CLOSING

I argue here for a new paradigm. One where mistakes are welcomed as evidence of innovation and as valuable opportunities for reflection and growth. One where we as a culture shy away from perfectionism and beating ourselves up and move instead toward self-acceptance and self-kindness. I believe this line of action will not only support teacher and student learning but will contribute to building a more compassionate and productive world.

A NOTE

Some of the narratives recounted in this volume are disquieting and some are downright distressing.

Since they are based on each individual's experiences and points of view, they necessarily exclude other points of view. Clearly, telling a single story from a single perspective obscures the complexity of the situation being represented.

These stories may sometimes require the reader to fill in the context and meaning with at best assumptions, and at worst stereotypes. The contributors to this volume were conscious that their stories could possibly reinforce rather than interrupt deficit stereotypes even as they sought to illuminate what are in most cases fairly typical errors and mistakes in judgment.

Any errors or oversight herein are my own. To say I'm thankful that the readers of this volume understand life as a process of learning and growth is an understatement.

Part I

DIVERSITY, EQUITY, AND INCLUSION

Chapter 1

Learning to Become Culturally Responsive

Teaching on an Indian Reservation

Anna Baldwin, EdD

Teacher at Arlee High School in Arlee, Montana,
located on the Flathead Indian Reservation
Course developer and teacher of Native American
Studies for the Montana Digital Academy
Adjunct Assistant Professor, University
of Montana—Missoula
2016 Classroom Teaching Ambassador Fellow
with the U.S. Department of Education
2014 Montana Teacher of the Year

Brand-new teachers fresh out of training programs are often told they have the tools needed to teach any students, any place they find a job. The teacher education courses they complete are full of information about special education law, methods of teaching literature such as fun book circles and drama-based projects, and what to do if one suspects a child has been neglected.

Though exceedingly nervous, coming out of a somewhat typical teacher training program, I felt confident that I could handle most of what a new teaching job could unearth. How could a new teacher anticipate the curve ball of cultural dissonance?

My first teaching job—the only one offered to me—was a position teaching high school English at an alternative school for Native American youth run by what was then called the Bureau of Indian Affairs (now the Bureau of Indian Education). This school served kids for whom the reservation's public school system was inadequate to meet their needs, often in ways tied to cultural features.

A rural school on a reservation with a majority non-Indian population due to agricultural and tourism opportunities, it is a unique and challenging place that revealed to me in just a month my woeful underpreparedness to address the students there.

Forrest Carter's *The Education of Little Tree* was my first book assignment for students. I deemed it a touching and culturally relevant book. The assigned classroom aide gently informed me that no, this novel and its author had been debunked as frauds. The "Indian" content was phony, and it would be better to choose a different title.

As a middle-class White woman from the East Coast, I knew absolutely nothing about reservations or tribal culture. Re-reading the book with this new knowledge about its author illuminated how he—and I—made too many assumptions, all of them poorly informed.

This incident with *Little Tree* exposed how little this teacher knew about the community that surrounded me: the homeland of the Salish, Kootenai, and Pend d'Oreille people plus all the tribal neighbors and others who had come to call this reservation home. My school had a cultural focus and instantly exposed the gaps in my own knowledge base. There were many gaps, and they were large.

Some tribal families hold deep and unresolved misgivings about public education and a historic mistrust of schools in general due to forced European-style schooling. One parent expressed that his parents *hid him* when the government men came around so he wouldn't be nabbed and carted off to boarding school. Another parent asked teachers to stop talking about a Blackfeet origin story, because his daughter's tribe had a longstanding conflict with it. In a very pointed experience, a student once said to the air between us, "How come this White lady is teaching me?"

Clearly, there would have been great benefit here to a teacher preparation experience focused on assessing the authenticity and quality of texts for Native American students, how to be a better cultural visitor, and how to alter one's assumptions. The need for content, pedagogy, and critical thinking skills to be able to see one's own bias and teach *around* it instead of *through* it was palpable.

But a teacher can tend to lean on a vision of a classroom made for kids like oneself.

A teacher who had come from stability, liked school, fit in fine, and believed in academic success as a way forward in life.

In short, without realizing it, I was asking the Native students in my school to be more like the White students I had been familiar with, like the White student I myself had been.

Over 80% of teachers are White, while the majority of students in our nation are not. That means that many new teachers will enter into workplaces as a cultural stranger. Perhaps colleges of education are better now at preparing their students for this reality than they were two decades ago, but given their track record of providing unhelpful training while avoiding crucial topics like cultural responsiveness, it is unlikely.

There are many reasons to avoid the mistakes described above. Not only is it better for the students and communities teachers serve for those teachers to be sensitive and informed, but it will save them the heartache and embarrassment of marching into a situation unprepared yet overconfident.

New teachers need to learn that most students are not like them in their dispositions, backgrounds, and motivations around school. Many new teachers enter schools with their own ideas of education: how students should act, how parents should respond, how schools should operate. In general, these preconceptions are based on the teachers' own experiences as students. In the reservation school, none of this applied.

Most new teachers wouldn't think to ask about these features during an interview; they are the underlying features of any school, not necessarily visible on websites or in statistics. It's only after two or three years that a new teacher might realize what exactly has caused so much chafing and tension, and either address it, or move on to another school which better fits their own teaching styles and needs.

Since most teachers are White, their experiences often do not reflect the culture of the students they will be teaching. This is true on reservations, in areas with high immigrant populations, in urban regions. It is increasingly true across the country. In rural America, where many towns are predominantly Caucasian, new teachers who land first jobs there often have no personal experience in rural areas, which have *their* own culture.

So, these new teachers must actively take the position of learner. They must humble themselves before the community they will serve, so that they can be taught.

Sometimes this instruction will be direct ("This author is a fraud"; "Stop teaching my child about Blackfeet origin stories") and sometimes it will be indirect ("How come this White lady is teaching me?"). Sometimes the new cultural information will be obvious: a student has to leave class suddenly because his cows got out; and sometimes it will be less so: half the school misses two weeks of class for a funeral.

The first years of teaching are difficult, exhausting, and can fill new teachers with self-doubt. The more unwilling a teacher is to admit they need help, the harder this work will be. New teachers should acknowledge how much help they need. Not only might they wrestle with classroom management, assignment type and length, and determining their persona as a teacher (mentor or instructor? Counselor or lecturer? Auntie or mom?), they might gain more traction faster if they recognize from the first moment of hiring the immense amount of learning they will need to do about their students themselves and the community they will serve.

Prior to their first hire, new teachers should learn to recognize their own biases and blind spots. They can put this step into action by turning to a resource such as the Harvard Bias Test which can help them identify their own privilege (or lack thereof) and beliefs about various cultural groups. Immediately upon first hire, conduct as much research as possible about their new school, including demographics, socioeconomic status, community resources and services, and teaching staff.

Plan lessons that meet the needs of students who will be in front of them, not the imaginary ones they have in their heads. One way to go about this: once in the classroom, pay close attention to the ways students receive their lessons—watch comments, body language, and read journal entries with care.

Two decades in, we should still be learning. We will still make mistakes. But if we can look before stepping, ask even if we think we're sure, turn to the experts whenever needed, and even occasionally when we don't think we need any outside input. Refer to people, texts, and other resources in order to ensure that the information one has is accurate. See the promise of students for who they are and not who you think they are.

FURTHER RESOURCES

Educators interested in learning more about how to identify bias in Native American texts can consult "How to Tell the Difference" [guide to identifying bias in Native American texts]. Oyate. 2018. http://oyate.org/index.php/resources/41-resources/how-to-tell-the-difference.

Harvard's Project Implicit Bias Test at https://implicit.harvard.edu/implicit/ is designed to help educators to see where they may hold implicit bias as the first step to working to mitigate their biases.

Teaching Tolerance offers a free online literacy-based anti-bias curriculum for K-12 called *Perspectives for a Diverse America* at their website tolerance.org. The National Education Association offers a number of resources to promote cultural competence at http://www.nea.org/home/39783.htm.

Chapter 2

Recognizing (Neuro)Diverse Perspectives in the English Language Arts Classroom

Christopher Bass
Teacher, Chicago Public Schools
Doctoral Candidate, University of Illinois, Chicago

Coming to recognize one's own ableist bias is a shocking and disheartening experience. Seeing just how an ableist bias has informed one's teaching—that space where ideas and constructs are perpetuated—is a devastating one.

But maybe it made sense. In doing research for a Humanities seminar in the cavernous university library, I stumbled upon a book with a ranking of states based on successful inclusion practices. My home state, Illinois, ranked near the bottom of the list.

Quietly closing the book and placing it back on its shelf, my mind remained restless, wanting to believe the words that described other teachers in other schools.

After all, how could one be a high school English teacher in Illinois for eight years, with nearly all of one's classes having at least one student with an Individualized Education Plan (IEP) or 504 plan and not be inclusive? How could a teacher have meticulously maintained the required IEP accommodations for students, be regarded as a successful inclusion teacher per administrative evaluations, and be replicating ableist approaches?

Ableism is a term used to describe discrimination based on assumptions around what makes a healthy body and normal mind. It perpetuates a belief that there is one "normal" way of living as a human. This ideology often emphasizes the *deficits* of differing abilities.

As a teacher of English, who worked with all forms of media, one rarely just naturally challenges the deficit portrayal of disability. If this is the case, though, a so-called inclusion classroom often unconsciously perpetuates ableist narratives around disability.

In order to disrupt the conventional culture of a school that had forged an ableist mentality around ability, one must decide to change both the type of texts used in the classroom and how the teacher and students use those texts.

The first step toward countering ableism in an ELA classroom is to integrate traditional model texts with contemporary texts written by neurodiverse authors. Critically reading these authors can lead both students and teachers to better understand the strengths and potential of difference.

Critically reading texts involves three key traits: First, consider how characters are portrayed, then challenge any stereotypes made in the portrayal of characters; discuss what cultures or communities are not present in the text and discuss the impact of the absence; finally, predict the author's intentions in writing the text.

Critically reading texts creates the classroom space for difference and in turn removes the stereotypes and assumptions around differing abilities. A broad textual representation of abilities disrupts the normative approaches to learning that usually push alternative possibilities and identities to the fringes of the classroom.

Neurodiversity is a term used to describe the variation of the human brain—in particular, one who claims to be "neurodiverse" identifies as having an atypical neurological condition such as dyslexia, dyscalculia, and autism. Students who identify as neurodiverse may have an IEP or 504 for a specific neurological condition and are heavily represented in inclusion classrooms across the United States. The malleable nature of the term *neurodiversity* highlights the varying assets connected with conditions that are too often pathologized via diagnosis.

An initial unit might pair, for example, two short memoirs each written by neurodiverse authors and containing neurodiverse characters. A teacher might choose pieces based on the conditions students in a particular class have IEPs for or which are commonly included under the umbrella of neurodiversity.

In introducing the pieces, a teacher should note that characters have abilities that many people might assume to be negatives and that these stories explore what it feels like to be judged for being different. The students can choose from either of the two authors.

All this is not to imply that establishing inclusivity is as easy as employing neurodiverse texts. When I employed this approach initially in my own classroom, I noted that in their reading journals, several students noted that they expected to find the characters "more relatable" because they understood what it felt like to be labeled as different.

Following the reading, a teacher can begin by assigning a student journal response about the readings. Ask students to respond to the texts using a variety of reader response questions that apply a disability studies theoretical lens: How do other people react to the protagonist's differences? Does either protagonist have a strength that that majority of people don't appreciate? Why might this be? How does society seem to create obstacles for the protagonist that might hinder her success? Can you relate to this story?

These journal questions should become the springboard for a class conversation that the teacher facilitates. However, once the conversation begins, it may become apparent that the students are unsure how to talk about the readings. The students may offer safe comments about generally appreciating the narrative voice, the humorous tone, and descriptions of the settings.

Facilitating discussion of neurodiversity can be tricky. In my experience, students are hesitant initially to mention anything about characters' disabilities. This discomfort likely stems from confusion about the concept of neurological diversity, so to ease student discomfort, explain that there are many different labels that fit within the definition of neurodiverse.

In my initial attempts at integrating neurodiverse literature, no matter how clear I thought I had made neurodiversity, the students did not seem to understand. This struggle led me to rely on simplistic, ableist jargon in an effort to better explain who may be considered neurodiverse.

I found myself defining conditions like autism, dyslexia, and anxiety. Though I tried to assure the class that neurodiversity is an inclusive category that breaks down divisions between diagnoses, I found it disturbingly easy to revert to the very labels that I wanted to avoid. And of course all the while, the students stared at me skeptically as I spoke.

In that initial class, one student eventually pointed out additional attributes of autism that I did not mention. She claimed to have done well on a research paper for biology and confidently asserted medical terms to describe the condition. Suddenly another student chimed in with the claim that her health teacher said depression was a "controllable" condition that should be medicated.

In response, I suggested that we turn to the text to consider how the authors had positive experiences with their neurodiversity. It was surprising that no students vocalized support for the positive portrayal of neurodiversity in the texts. At the bell, those students with IEPs silently walked out of the classroom with looks of embarrassment after being diagnosed and defined by their peers.

I had failed.

It was difficult to admit that my original plan did not work. However, my reflections, the student writing, and classroom discussions all proved that we had failed to move beyond ableist assumptions. This realization occurred after some difficult honest assessment of the classwork. While critical literacy led to revealing conversations, the students never embodied a more inclusive approach to learning.

In many ways, these conversations merely uncovered power indifferences without making any changes to them. It certainly didn't feel empowering. Yet, at the same time, an inclusive environment was too important to give up on. As the teacher, I needed to find differing methods.

My experience trying to build an inclusive environment highlights the difficulties general education teachers often face while deconstructing barriers. In an attempt to create an inclusive classroom, I turned toward the material I know best—the literature and methods of my content. However, while I made my curricular content more inclusive through neurodiverse characters and authors, I failed to recognize the exclusive aspects of both my teaching methods and the design of my classroom.

After that first failure, it became clear that inclusive teaching must expand beyond mere shifts in content material. Though the *material* became more inclusive, inclusive teachers must make interacting with these texts more accessible for all learners. As a result, inclusive pedagogy demands a redesign of both the classroom's physical layout and the pedagogical pacing to assure instruction becomes more flexible for all learners.

Inclusive teaching begins on the first day of the new semester. All students should be encouraged to identify individual strengths and abilities that have gone unrecognized in previous classes.

In addition to the student comments, it is important to review IEP and 504 plans; however, often these documents emphasize student deficits, so inclusive teachers may also follow up with colleagues in special education, student's parents, and other allies to learn more about the abilities and strengths of these students. Though this step takes time, it leads to more productive, inclusive learning in the classroom and fosters a friendly connection between parents and colleagues, which can be helpful as the year progresses.

Following this first step, in the following weeks, inclusive teachers create a more fluid instructional space to maximize the student strengths, which were shared in earlier conversations. A shift toward flexibility also begins with the teacher's language. Teachers should emphasize asset-based language. For example, encourage student writing to be "atypical" and celebrate student writing models that seem "divergent" from their peers. All writing workshops may begin with a reminder that there is no "normal" approach to writing and responding to texts.

Students often respond positively to this shift in language. In the end of semester reflections, a student of mine noted, "I felt encouraged to be myself" because of the established "welcoming environment."

In addition to asset-based diction choices, inclusive educators must also adjust the physical layout of the classroom. Each shift in the classroom layout should promote student abilities and maximize the potential for student success. Inclusive pedagogy may be sparked by various adjustments, such as the following:

- Altered arrangement of desks and seating charts to maximize student access and collaboration.
- Dimming of fluorescent lighting to avoid overstimulating students.
- Accounting for wheelchair users and classroom aides in classroom setup.
- Making extra handouts easily accessible for students who may have trouble with attendance.

Keep in mind, too, that classroom spaces may not be an ideal learning environment for independent work, so allow students to work in the hallway, library, or other quiet space when needed.

In addition to making the physical space more accessible, inclusive pedagogy requires that teachers become more flexible in curriculum design.

To work toward a more inclusive curriculum, teachers can employ the following:

- Allowing students to leave the room when needed.
- Support for students to communicate via email or online discussion boards rather than only in classroom conversations, which can make a few students anxious.
- Free movement: Certain students with ADHD may benefit from the freedom to move around the classroom when needed.
- Closed captioning on all videos (most students benefit from this!).
- Rolling deadlines: Students with anxiety may have higher success when deadlines are loosened for students with anxiety.

Similarly, all students benefit from consistent assignment revision policies.

These inclusive approaches toward instruction and classroom design can have a positive impact on the ways students collaborate and seek help among each other. There is a sense of shared purpose among the students. In a successful inclusive space, students also become more empathetic and refrain from judging students whose writing process may seem atypical.

As a result of these shifts toward inclusivity, no one stands out because the relaxation of rules enables each student to do what personally works best. Moreover, these steps toward inclusive teaching create a space in which students continually experiment with what might work best for them. This leads to greater risk-taking in student writing.

Inclusive education is responsive to the individual strengths of students, communities, and teachers, and inclusive practices vary per classroom. This is the challenge of inclusive work—there is no singular framework. It can only begin when a teacher recognizes the disabling nature of institutions and demands equality of all abilities.

FURTHER RESOURCES

Teachers interested in working toward more inclusive pedagogy may find materials in Universal Design for Learning (UDL) and the scholarship of the Disability Studies in Education (DSE) community helpful.

Danforth's (2014) text, *Becoming a Great Inclusive Educator*, helpfully outlines the theories of DSE as well as providing ideas to approach inclusive work.

Similarly, Baglieri's (2017) text, *Disability Studies and the Inclusive Classroom: Critical Practices for Embracing Diversity in Education*, is the kind of text that should be included in all teacher-training programs. Baglieri recommends specific approaches to teaching that best align with the values of DSE.

Finally, Robert Rozema's text, *Seeing the Spectrum: Teaching Autistic Adolescents through the English Language Arts*, is an excellent resource for asset-based approaches to teaching autism.

Chapter 3

Manuel's T-shirt

Learning a Hard Lesson about Student Poverty

Kip Téllez, PhD

Professor, Department of Education
University of California, Santa Cruz

My first teaching position, 35 years ago, was located in an elementary school in an unincorporated part of eastern Los Angeles County. The community was not unfamiliar to me, but every neighborhood and school has its own constellation of beliefs, values, and behaviors, and there was much to learn, especially about the poverty the students' families experienced, particularly those who were also the children of immigrants.

I was well prepared for teaching, or so I thought, but working with forty fifth and sixth graders in a combination class, whose native languages included Spanish, Vietnamese, Egyptian Arabic, Samoan, and Tagalog, tested me in ways I never thought possible.

The school was in a community not far from my own home, and, as the child of teachers, I figured I knew enough about doing without the expensive things other, more middle- and upper-class kids had, and that I would be able to relate well to these lower income students. As I found out, I had much to learn, and my formative experience and my professional growth in this regard was a painful lesson.

His name was Manuel, and like most immigrant students, he was very hardworking. Even as a fifth grader, he was still in need of additional English skills though, especially reading and writing. His mathematics achievement was near the top of the class, and he prided himself on completing his work on time and with great accuracy. Manuel showed me how his father taught him to do mathematics problems based on his education in Mexico.

One morning Manuel arrived at school wearing a UCLA t-shirt, which I immediately noticed.

The UCLA mascot is a bruin, a Dutch term for bear, and Manuel's shirt sported a snarling version with the letters UCLA below. The shirt appeared to be slightly worn, as if an older brother had passed it on to him. To that point at the school, I had not seen any students wear anything that represented a college, so I quickly peppered him with questions. Did he want to go to UCLA for college? Did he know someone who had gone there? Had he watched the UCLA football team on television?

Manuel looked at me, baffled by my questions. He did not respond, but just smiled back at me the kind of sheepish smile someone makes when they are uncomfortable. I guessed, wrongly, that Manuel had not understood my questions, which was not altogether an unreasonable assumption since he was an English learner, or what we called back then, an ESL (English as a Second Language) student.[1]

Then, after a few more of my questions went unanswered, I doubled down, as if my intention was to humiliate him, and I asked the whole class about their college plans. I expressed that I was so excited that Manuel was a fan of UCLA, and that he and the others should set their sights high and do all they could to attend this prestigious university, or any university for that matter.

On and on I droned about the importance of college, and with each mention of Manuel's name, he grew more red. Why was he embarrassed? I was praising him in front of the whole class for his smart choice in a t-shirt. And I thought about how I, Mr. Awesome Beginning Teacher, was taking advantage of the legendary "teachable" moment.

Manuel's discomfort was not allayed by the rest of the students' deeper understanding of UCLA; they had only the vaguest notion of a university. A few mentioned that their parents wanted them to go to college, but they had no idea where or how it was going to happen. And none had heard of UCLA, even though the campus was just thirty miles from the school.

Recess came and I was able to reflect on my inspirational speech, and as Manuel was leaving the room, I found yet another opportunity to make him really uncomfortable and asked, "So where did you get the shirt?" By this point, he was visibly upset, and he looked down and mumbled, "I don't know. My mom just got it for me."

Then I realized, in a moment of stark disgrace (for now it was my turn), how and why Manuel had come by that shirt. In college, my friends and I would often make the rounds of thrift or used clothing stores, trying to find 1960s-era clothes that matched the "new wave" style popular at the time, which is another, although less disgraceful, part of my past. As we rummaged through the bins, I was always shocked at how many college clothes were given away to such stores, and I now realized where Manuel got his.

Perhaps he was shopping with his family and just liked the cartoonish bear on the front. Or perhaps it was the shirt in the best condition for the price, and his mom told him to wear it. It was the longest recess in my life; I just sat at my desk trying to figure out how to redeem Manuel's dignity while kicking myself for being so unaware.

Of course Manuel didn't want to tell me or his classmates where he got the shirt. He didn't know anything about UCLA. Why would he? His parents had immigrated from a rural part of Michoacan, Mexico, thousands of miles from UCLA. He was the oldest child in his family, so it would have been impossible for an older sibling to have given him the shirt.

After recess, Manuel returned to the class and then looked at me, his face now showing trepidation, his smile turning to anxious glances. He probably feared a reprise of the absurd discussion of his shirt. I walked over to him and quietly said, "I like your shirt," hoping the intonation in my sentence signaled to Manuel that I was done talking about it.

In that moment I realized that I had to better understand how my students and their families managed to make ends meet. My own upbringing had not prepared me, and I wanted to make sure I never humiliated a student as I had Manuel.

A current challenge for schools—and one that appears to be long lasting— is the relationship between the culture of the teacher and the culture of the students. For many years, this was of little concern to anyone. It was simply assumed that teachers, as representatives of the dominant culture, would impart their cultural values and beliefs to the students, irrespective of how those beliefs conflicted with those of the students.

We have, with good reason, come to question our earlier neglect of this relationship, asking perhaps if the cultural mismatch between the teacher and the students could prevent *all* students, especially those from different cultural and economic backgrounds, from achieving to their highest capabilities.

Poverty is not the same as culture, and teachers should avoid talking about poverty as a culture or "the culture of poverty." Poverty is a condition, not a culture. Culture is not necessarily fixed, but it's far more permanent than poverty.

For instance, families can move in and out of poverty but retain their cultural heritage. As a Mexican-American, I had a cultural window into some of my students, but many represented cultural groups that were unfamiliar to me. But for nearly all of them, they faced economic hardships that were not part of their teacher's experience, such as shopping at thrift stores for everyday clothes.

A teacher must learn about the economic conditions of students. But where to start? I knew that staying within the walls of the school was a fruitless strategy; I had to get "outside."

I decided against the "anthropologist" strategy, whereby teachers invite themselves into the homes of the students and then take careful "field notes" of what they find there. This idea, sometimes called gaining access to students' "funds of knowledge," has been promoted by many educators. This approach has merit, but I have never felt comfortable inviting myself into someone's home, regardless of my position.

A better strategy is to start conversations with students that encourage them to share their lives outside of school. For example, after asking one boy about his soccer team, I asked if I could attend one of his games. That started a wave of invitations to baseball games, church confirmations, quinciñeras, Tet celebrations, and other social events, some even to the families' homes, where I was welcomed as a genuine guest.

After a year or so of seeing my students and their families outside of school, I learned how resourceful they were, but also that the poverty some of them faced was soul crushing.

Alter your instruction based on what you learn. For instance, I learned that nearly all of the Mexican-descent families sent a significant portion of their income to family members still in Mexico. These "remittances" were considered obligatory, and had to be factored in when the family was making decisions about money. I used the concept to teach percent.

And with Manuel's t-shirt in mind, I also went to the thrift stores in the area and looked for the children's clothing I might see in my classroom. I also visited "La Pulga" (the flea market) in town, where many of the students spent their Saturdays helping their families sell items they had made or cooked.

You might find that although most families struggle, you'll see others doing quite well. After the father got a promotion or the mother completed a nursing program, for instance, they were able to buy a house and move from the school attendance zone, which was made up largely of rentals. I was conflicted when economic success for one of our school's families often meant moving to a different, and often higher performing, school.

But my experience with Manuel's t-shirt taught me never to assume that my students knew the meaning behind what they wore or brought to school. In my nine years of working at the school, I learned to simply say, "Cool shirt. I can tell you what it's about if you want me to." Sometimes they wanted an explanation, sometimes not, but they always liked it when I complimented their clothes.

FURTHER RESOURCES

Teachers interested in learning about students' and their families' economic resources can also use the U.S. census (https://www.census.gov/en.html) to find statistical information (e.g., poverty rates, home values) on their school's neighborhoods.

Local officials, such as county supervisors, city council members, district pupil services directors, or school board trustees, might also be able to share useful information. In particular, these local agencies often know the rates of homelessness among youth in their region.

In fact, California school districts are now given additional state funding for the number of homeless students they enroll, so careful records must be kept. Statistical information can inform what teachers know about their students, but there is no substitute for direct experience. As the anthropologist Ruth Landes wrote, "Separateness from the objects of discussion forfeits the experience that words should mirror."

NOTE

1. We continue to struggle with the terms that define students who are learning English. In the United States, it is still irritatingly common to hear some educators

refer to a student as "LEP," or limited English proficient. This federal designation sounds ugly ("leper" or "lip") and, more important, points our attention to what the student does not know. Like many ELD educators, I have tried to support other, more positive terms and argued that our students were best referred to as "emerging bilinguals," a term that I believe both emphasizes the developmental aspect of teaching and learning and made clear that all students have a native language and are now gaining a new one. After a few years of trying to convince my graduate students and colleagues to adopt the "emerging bilingual" label, I gave up. Although I still think my term has merit and others have recently used one similar ("emergent" bilinguals).

Chapter 4

Semantic Snafu

How I Learned to Choose My Words Carefully

Chris Anson, PhD
Distinguished University Professor and Director
of Campus Writing and Speaking Program
North Carolina State University

"I demand that you stop using that example," the young woman said tensely, gesticulating toward the materials scattered on the large presentation table as the other students filed out of the lecture hall.

Many years ago, I was regularly teaching a high-enrollment course called "Introduction to English Language and Linguistics" at a major research-oriented university. The course satisfied an undergraduate elective category and was also required of all Education majors, so it routinely enrolled over 200 students who filled one of the capacious lecture halls on campus.

The course constituted a broad introduction to the English language. As such, it included units on the linguistic aspects of English (phonology, morphology, syntax, semantics, and pragmatics), as well as material on social and regional English dialects, a brief history of the language, child language development, the psychology of language, and the development of writing systems. It was a tough course.

Students were not used to studying language scientifically, and usually around 7 to 8 percent of them failed, which motivated me to provide as much support as possible.

To make matters worse, the course was delivered in an inhospitable learning environment, with rows of tiered desks bolted to the floor and a large presentation area in front with projection equipment for lecturing. As a result, it was important to keep students engaged through active-learning strategies.

Almost every class included short breakouts. In pairs or small groups, the students analyzed raw language data using linguistic methods, such as looking for the distribution of phonemes, applying tools of syntax to complex sentences, or studying samples of children's speech.

Or they discussed ethical questions such as the implications of taking an accommodationist, erradicationist, or bidialectal view of African American English. Or they briefly shared reflections that they were writing almost daily in a required learning log.

One such breakout usually occurred after students had worked through the linguistic building blocks of English, and made for a good summary activity before moving on to dialectology. Using the best display technology at the time—an overhead transparency—I projected a string of humorously ambiguous newspaper headlines.

The small groups were tasked with analyzing the linguistic source of the ambiguity in each headline: Was it syntactic? Semantic? Phonological? Some combination? Who or what was the agent? They would set to work, and the room was always soon abuzz with laughter and productive talk.

- *Iraqi head seeks arms*
- *Baseball talks in ninth inning*
- *Kicking baby considered to be healthy*
- *President wins on budget, but more lies ahead*
- *Robber holds up Albert's hosiery*
- *One witness told police she had seen sexual intercourse taking place between two parked cars*
- *Kids make nutritious snacks*
- *Neanderthal man barbecued*
- *President enters Dinah Shore [golf tournament]*
- *Terminal smog may not be lethal*
- *Columnist gets urologist in trouble with his peers*
- *Giant panda gives birth to baby boy*
- *Survivor of Siamese twins joins parents*

During one term, after this activity ended and the class adjourned, a student named Sarah approached the front of the room. Sarah always sat in the first or second row of the lecture hall, was highly attentive during the class sessions, and asked excellent questions. She had already received very high quiz scores, and wrote long, exploratory entries in her learning log.

Sarah seemed quite agitated. After I had greeted her pleasantly, she took on an authoritative demeanor. "I demand that you stop using that example," she snapped. "Actually, I want the name and contact information of the publisher that created your overheads."

I explained that the transparencies were my creations. (I was obsessed with designing elegant overheads, thanks to a decent computer and special printer-ready acetates in my department.) "I like to tailor-make everything in my courses," I said with a hint of pride that soon changed to concern. "But what example are you talking about?"

"One of those headlines from today's class," she replied. "It's highly objectionable to me."

After I had retrieved the overhead from the stack on the table, Sarah pointed directly to the Dinah Shore item. "That one," she said. She went on to explain that she was a feminist separatist and was extremely disturbed by the image rendered in the headline. "This is a phallogocentric piece of . . . language that's about violent male dominance," she declared. "It has no place in a course about the English language—or any course. The image is shocking to me."

Taken aback, I assured her that in no way was the example meant to offend anyone; in fact, it commonly appeared in lists of funny headline gaffes. But as student-centered as I was and have always been, I promised to toss the headline and not use it again in my courses. "Sarah, if even one student objects with good reason to something I do or say, it disappears from my course," I told her with conviction. "But let's look through the rest, just in case."

As we glanced through the headlines, I asked whether the headline about the parked cars was also troubling. "Nope," she replied. "That one's OK." "Any others?" I asked. "No," she said, scanning the list again. "The rest are fine."

Satisfied, she collected her things and left. As my teaching assistant and I walked back to the building where our department was located, I told her about the encounter with Sarah and asked her frank opinion. "I guess I can see why it might bother some people," she said, "but it didn't really cross my mind until now."

Later that day, I sent an almost effusive email to Sarah thanking her for calling attention to an objectionable example in the course and repeating my promise to permanently remove the headline from the overhead transparency. "I'm very sorry that this item disturbed you, Sarah," I wrote, "and please alert me about anything else that you or other students find objectionable."

Sarah was right, I thought as I reflected on the headline. How would the class discuss its ambiguity, anyway? They'd have to be explicit about the double-entendre, which could make some students uncomfortable. I suddenly realized that I'd never asked for a large-group follow-up of this item when we reconvened; I always selected a few headlines for the groups to report on because there wasn't time to discuss them all.

Tacitly, I'd kept the Dinah Shore example from consideration.

Why was it there to begin with? After all, I had rejected any number of other possible headlines.

Was I unconsciously imagining that some students—maybe more men than women—would be titillated by the example and therefore more "engaged"? Had I generalized my students somehow or lost sight of their diversity? As a cisgendered male, had I been indifferent or oblivious to the range of possible responses?

The next morning, my inbox contained a brief response from Sarah, thanking me for accommodating her complaint. "That's all I needed," she explained. "No need to flagellate yourself over it. These things happen, and I'm just especially sensitive to them. I appreciate your accommodation."

I stared at the email. *Flagellate*. Latin, from the seventeenth century. "To whip or scourge." The whip image originates in the nominal root of the word, *flagellum,* the lash-like appendage that gives sperm their motility. But more: the violent image of early radical Christians who *flagellated* themselves, mortifying the flesh by lashing their backs with a scourge, usually with three tails sometimes affixed with nails.

A *flagellant* is someone who subjects themselves or others to flogging for either religious or sexual purposes. I'd long before avoided the word in casual usage because of its objectionable history, the same as words and phrases like "rule of thumb," "Dutch treat," "old wives' tale," "Scot-free," and "retard" (as a general epithet).

But what to do? At first it seemed that this was a case of forgivable igno-rance, not that Sarah had chosen the word deliberately. After all, she was an undergraduate in a survey course, not a language expert. But she was also among the brightest and well-prepared students in the class. Wouldn't she have some knowledge of the word's meaning and history?

Sarah had rightfully questioned an image created through the use of the word "enters," and I capitulated, caught in an instructional mistake. Now I was questioning images (spermatozoa, self-inflicted whipping) that Sarah had created through the use of the word "flagellate," based on what I believed would be her own objections.

But how was it possible to know whether, in fact, she would object? How much was clear about her worldview to predict her reaction? Would revealing these etymological facts look like some sort of retribution for challenging my selection of content? Or was she in the know and was testing my own tolerance for objectionable words? And if so—if her teacher didn't respond to her use of the word—would it betray an ignorance in an area of his expertise?

Or if I did respond, would she appreciate a new insight, and be even more committed to studying language and to using it carefully? Would I be making a second mistake with her, or furthering the cause of linguistic sensitivity that she began with? If I let it go and she was uninformed, would anyone ever call attention to the linguistic facts, or would she go through her life unaware of the word's source and never have the opportunity to decide whether it was objectionable to her?

And all this was happening in a *course* on language—a course that included etymological activities. Students studied the roots of interesting words and expressions. Through mini-scenarios, they judged controversies such as whether *niggardly*, a word from Old Norse meaning stingy or penurious, should be banned or avoided because it resembles a highly objectionable word with an altogether different source and meaning.

In such a course, didn't I have an obligation to inform and educate Sarah?

For some time I pondered these questions in light of my initial mistake, and then reached a decision.

FURTHER RESOURCES

This scenario raises issues about appropriate language use in classrooms, but indirectly it also speaks to more general issues of classroom climate and the inclusion of all students through choice of words, tone, visuals, directives, and most other elements of classroom teaching.

Classrooms that alienate students or make them feel unjustifiably uncomfortable may negatively affect their learning. An excellent resource on inclusive teaching is the website of the Derek Bok Center for Teaching and Learning at Harvard University: https://bokcenter.harvard.edu/inclusive-teaching.

The University of Michigan's Center for Research on Teaching and Learning also has a web page of resources on inclusive teaching, with a blog that regularly features topics such as "teaching in the current political climate," "assessing and addressing our biases," and "responding to incidents of hate speech": http://www.crlt.umich.edu/multicultural-teaching/inclusive-teaching-strategies.

Part II

REFRAMING ASSUMPTIONS

Chapter 5

Grading and Gatekeeping

Andy Boyle
Instructional Technology Specialist
Kennesaw State University iTeach

As an economics teacher, I was a gatekeeper of sorts. After all, *my* class was a graduation requirement. To get that diploma, students had to do well in my class, and I took pride in that fact.

By the time I was in my third year of teaching, all of my previous teaching experience had been in urban schools with "at-risk" students (a term in the current parlance at the time). My students were mostly young people of color from low socioeconomic backgrounds, and I saw my mission as their teacher as "saving" them from their conditions.

This empathy manifested itself in rigid expectations around completing my assignments and participating while in my classroom. And so clearly, attendance was paramount for me. After all, I was delivering lectures that I expected would totally prepare my students for the make-or-break End of Course Exam.

So of course when Mark, a senior intending to graduate, stopped showing up part-way through spring semester, I was concerned.

That was my third year, and I was not teaching in an urban school any longer, but in a totally different context, one that I didn't have familiarity with: a school in a hunting and fishing community. My students were now mostly white and from middle-class backgrounds, and the school itself had a high percentage of first-time high school graduates. It's hard to say with certainty now, but maybe that strengthened my resolve about enforcing my expectations for my students.

I noticed, though, that once fishing season opened, student attendance dropped. Mark was absent almost every day. I dutifully called his mother the Friday before spring break.

"Mark has over 30 absences out of the 60 class meetings for my economics class," I explained. "He won't walk for graduation without passing my class, and I can't pass a student with this many absences," I said to her, pleading my case.

His mother seemed to understand the import of the situation. Regardless, after coming back from spring break, Mark continued to miss days.

When it came time to take the End of Course Exam, Mark surprisingly was present, and he scored a 93 on the test.

I couldn't accept, though, that he could have scored a nearly perfect score on that important, high-stakes test with such spotty attendance and without completing so many of my assignments.

I accused him of cheating without any evidence.

It was a reasonable assumption in many ways. He had missed almost all of the in-class activities and lectures. And he sat for the computerized test next to one of my best students.

My grading approach at the time was such that I didn't count zeros in the gradebook against my students. That would work to Mark's advantage, since his entry in my gradebook had more zeros than a line of computer code. But I just didn't feel as though Mark had *enough* grades in the gradebook to pass my class, even if the grades he *did* have (once I dropped all the zeros) were good ones. He had missed several summative assessments, too. Mark hadn't demonstrated to me that he had met the state standards for high school economics.

Mark offered to do make-up work in the form of a project at the end of the year in an effort to salvage his meager efforts in high school economics. But I did what I felt Mark had set me up to do—I failed him.

This time, Mark's mom showed a lot of concern about his economics grade, and berated me over the phone and by way of a nasty email. Mark's grandparents had already booked their flights for graduation to see him walk. He was supposed to be the first high school graduate in the family. I had a tense meeting with the principal as a result of all this as well.

In spite of all this, Mark ended up graduating. After completing the economics course in summer school, he graduated in August instead of with his senior class. I still felt steadfast in the decision I'd made. I was teaching Mark an important life lesson. At the time, I hadn't developed an understanding of cultural norms, community expectations, or even how to modulate what was really important in terms of being successful, happy people and how my teaching might lead directly or indirectly to those outcomes.

Mark went on to be quite happy, in spite of this blemish on his academic record. At the time of writing, he is engaged, has two children, and is a college graduate and a productive, working member of society.

I left the classroom in 2010 and started working with teachers on education technology implementation. With this came a broadened perspective. I could see, finally, beyond the microcosm of my own classroom and curriculum and could think about teaching and learning across the nodes of a myriad of classrooms and course content across disciplines.

And I have come to feel strongly that empathy and compassion is more important than anything else in the realm of schooling. I was talking recently to a physical education teacher who bragged about failing elementary students for not dressing out for his class. "I don't want to minimize your influence and your role," I said to him. "But can they do what they need to do in your class in their jeans?" I think, maybe kids don't have clean clothes to change into for P.E. class. Maybe their parents are working two jobs and aren't home long enough to do the laundry and still get some sleep.

As I write this, I'm sheltered in place because of a pandemic. Schools are closed and students are at home trying to learn in a variety of contexts, and they are contexts they can't control. Teachers don't know, for the most part, what students are experiencing at home.

Inequalities with regard to internet connections in the home when schools go full-remote or access to devices on which to learn have come into stark relief. These are issues I've long worked on in my role supporting the thoughtful uptake of educational technology, but I am coming to understand them in a new way.

Early in my career, I thought I was empathic because I had high standards for my students and was steadfast about the best way to hold students to those standards. But I see empathy and compassion in a new way now with the benefit of hindsight.

Those new to the field can't easily realize the affordances of hindsight, but there are in-roads for shifting your point of view in ways that can mimic the kind of perspective you gain as you progress in your career.

Seek advice from an experienced teacher you trust. Swallow your pride and seek out advice. Ask for help. Had I asked another teacher in the school about the context in which Mark was experiencing schooling, I would have likely gained a quick understanding of community standards and expectations around attendance (and graduation).

Take advantage, too, of the instructional and social coaches in your building, if available. Reflection is a central piece of instructional coaching and, regrettably, it's missing from too many teachers' experiences. We are so busy there is rarely enough time to run to the restroom let alone to reflect on our own practice.

If teachers don't have the advantages of in-building coaches, videotaping classroom instruction can be a useful proxy. Even posing the most basic of questions while watching the playback such as "what are kids doing in my class?" will prove illuminating. We think and feel as teachers that something specific is happening in our classrooms. Watching the video of a class can support reflective practice in powerful ways.

At the time of this writing, our state is rethinking grading in a way that has perhaps inspired this reflection. No one fails, and the minimum grade one can dole out is a 70. Some schools are identifying junior and senior repeaters missing a class or two for graduation and enrolling them in those classes so they get the course credits and graduate.

If high school is not working for some students, why are we trying so hard to keep them in high school?

In ten years we will be able to see all the ways in which these very students prevail in the system that was designed to hold them back. I'll be cheering them on when I see that they're productive, or have families, or are just happy in ways that are big or small.

If they're happy, we will know the true impact of our work as teachers—whether they were supported in chasing their dreams, or if school slowed them down and played a role that proved to be the opposite of their intention when they showed up in our classroom. Day to day, we take what we are doing very seriously. But life is much bigger. Much grander.

FURTHER RESOURCES

Educators interested in learning more about how grading systems can perpetuate inequality can survey Joe Feldman's *Grading for Equity: What It Is, Why*

It Matters, and How It Can Transform Schools and Classrooms and work by Alfie Kohn including *The Case Against Standardized Testing.*

Educators can search recent studies on student retention and life outcomes for students to learn about the negative impact grade retention may have on students.

Chapter 6

On Teaching and Toolsheds

Role Reversal on the Construction Site

Mike Land, PhD
Director, Community Service-Learning Program
Associate Professor, English
Assumption College

Like most English professors, I began teaching undergraduate writing classes as soon as I entered grad school. While those undergrads might have felt short-changed by not having a "real professor," I told myself this situation was good for them. Not only were they getting someone striving to mold himself into the best possible teacher—one worthy of a tenure-track job someday—but they were also working with a prof who still knew what it was like to be in their shoes.

There was one problem with that proposition. While I was a graduate student in workshops filled with people whose passion was writing, I was teaching undergraduates whose passions, well, lay elsewhere.

Which brings us to Lloyd.

I liked Lloyd (not his real name) well enough. I thought I was OK with the fact that he said very little from his spot on the back row of my intermediate composition class. But when reading his papers, it was hard to resist invoking the same vocabulary I'd often heard in graduate-level workshops, critiques that seemed to equate bad writing with moral flaws.

His writing was "passive" and "lazy," lacking "focus" and "concentration." I didn't actually use those words in my comments, but I thought that way about his writing, which obviously then had an impact on both my expectations and, of course, his grade.

In my class with Lloyd, I kept right on teaching that way until the halfway point of the semester—when I took the risk of leading my students into the world beyond the campus. A former journalist, I believed students should experience the power of writing about an off-campus venture we shared together—and that the experience shouldn't just be a field trip in which we'd be reduced to mere tourists.

I wanted them to strive—and to succeed, or fail, or both—and write about that experience.

So I scheduled our class to take part in a community service-learning project at a Habitat for Humanity building site. Having done my share of Habitat projects over the years, I'd expected we'd blend into a larger group of volunteers who would tell us what to do every step of the way. This, I figured, would mask how little I knew about how to build even the simplest thing.

Like Lloyd on the back row, I was hoping to hide.

Instead, the foreman called our class into the backyard, looked into my eyes, and announced, "I want you to build the family a shed."

A free-standing structure. From scratch.

We were to do this with no blueprint—not that I could've read one. Instead, there was just a crude diagram the guy sketched on a scrap of paper, with all the formal detail of someone drawing up a backyard football play in the dirt.

My students stared at their new foreman. Me.

One of the underlying assumptions of teaching is that teachers are supposed to project a sense of mastery. It's certainly a reasonable expectation for our students, who—along with their parents—are paying dearly for a quality product. Hey, we pay dearly for that appearance of credibility ourselves, part of the cost being that our loan debt from grad school might rival that of our undergrads.

Plus, in that fake-it-until-you-make-it way of adapting to a new profession, we have to project that sense of mastery and authority as we jump through the hoops to a tenure-track job, then to tenure itself. Along the way, we learn to make everyone who depends on us feel that they're getting what they paid for.

So we hang our diplomas on our walls, so we make allusions to grad school, so—if your qualifications rest on your previous career—you make references to your own days in the field, all to reinforce the authority that students expect us to be. Given all that hard work on the image, it's tempting to avoid pedagogical situations that might shatter the illusion that you always know what you're doing.

Yet that professional ethic went against so much of what wisdom that the real world offered. Back in Alabama in the 1980s—when I was a newspaper reporter who often came to work not knowing what story I would research, write, and publish in the next 24 hours—deeper lessons were about having to continuously adapt and improvise once the initial plan went awry.

Once I made fun of a pop celebrity's publicity photo on my editor's desk, only to have the editor laugh and tell me she was "glad you have this sardonic attitude, because you've got to interview her in 15 minutes." Indeed, one of my most important skills was how to report and write my way around obstacles, pulling one iron after another out of the fire.

Sure, I would get burned along the way. But I developed faith in my ability to adapt, to worry less about the just-past mistake, to reject the notion that the goal was to avoid errors altogether.

The same lessons applied to my personal community service back in the 1980s. I helped found one non-profit in which we, like academics, moved forward with care and deliberation. But thanks to one of our presidents, we also learned that there were times to "create a crisis." To set a bold goal, then scramble to meet it. Sure, you'll probably fall short of that perfect ideal—but you'll come closer than you ever dreamed.

My "create a crisis" friend would've chafed at the glacial pace of academia. But he would've liked my colleagues who fearlessly apply the experiential education that is Community Service-Learning—also known at various colleges as Civic or Community Engagement, Community-Based Learning, or other terms in the continual redefinition festival that is academia.

No matter what you call it, teachers who design and implement such components are driven by an idealistic vision of what the educational experience should be for students—as well as what educational institutions owe to the community that hosts them. Of course, every entity you add to such a partnership just heightens the chance of something going wrong. But the good that comes of these ventures is well worth all the crises that occur along the way.

One of my most visionary colleagues, a Spanish professor who creates elaborate creative collaborations with refugees, sent me a long email on Christmas weekend, laying out all the networking setbacks in a course he would start teaching in a matter of weeks. The problems he detailed would be seen by the control freaks amongst us as an excellent reason never to put one's course at the mercy of the unpredictable broader world. By the email's end, though, my friend's mood shifted from panic to positivity. "Oh well," he declared, "I'm optimistically clueless."

"Optimistic cluelessness" became a fixture in my annual State of CSL talk at my college. Yes, I reminded my colleagues, we should do everything we can to design experiences well in advance. But we also must learn to trust in the power of mutual vulnerability, the ability of both teachers and students to come together when something doesn't go right.

Mistakes aren't something to be avoided at all costs. They're practically part of the design.

Certainly, they're part of the learning opportunity not only for the students but also for the instructors.

But two decades earlier, back at the construction site, I hadn't yet worked all this out. I hadn't embraced the faith of "optimistic cluelessness"—although I was certainly feeling plenty of the latter. I just looked blankly at the construction supervisor, feeling the weight of my students' expectations upon me.

In a matter of seconds, I would be exposed for the fraud I was. They would know I didn't deserve to be a professor. They would be even more sure that my fallback career wasn't going to be carpentry.

Perhaps it was the length of my pause, or the blankness of my stare, but finally a student shouldered his way into the conversation.

It was, of all people, Lloyd.

He asked the construction site foreman a question I'd never have known to ask, and got an answer I didn't know to apply. In the matter of a few seconds, Lloyd became the person the foreman looked in the eye, while I joined the ranks of the classmates trying to follow the plan the two experts were laying out for us.

As the foreman walked away, Lloyd must've noticed my raised eyebrows. He shrugged and grinned.

"My dad's a subcontractor," he said.

Then he turned to his classmates, also known as my former students.

"So can anyone find a carpenter's square?"

"What's a carpenter's square?" a student asked—saving me the trouble.

I was more than happy to let Lloyd do the teaching for the rest of the long, hot day. When I wasn't hoisting two-by-fours at his command, I was herding more passive students. Ironically, in this new setting, while Lloyd was working with both vigor and confidence, the star writers who dominated so much of the classroom discussion were hanging back, unsure of themselves.

His writing seemed to improve after that day, as did his participation. At the time, I attributed this to the confidence he gained from his raised stature in the class—as well as the chance to construct sentences about construction, the kind of building that actually puts roofs, and not just metaphors, above people's heads.

But I suspect the truth was that I'd simply misread Lloyd's performance all along. Perhaps I should have taken my students to the construction site from the very start. For in succumbing to institutional pressure to adopt the mentality of the grader anxious to prove he was tough enough—rather than that of advocate intent on engaging the student where he was—I'd failed to engage Lloyd as a whole person, with his own work ethic and talents to bring to the table.

In the future, I'd learn to build in more opportunities for individual connection with the students—discussions that weren't just about the academic task at hand. I'd also work even harder at creating chances for the student to bring their broader range of skills to bear to the work at hand, building confidence that academic inquiry has relevance to their broader world and that they, in turn, have something to contribute to academics.

And while it doesn't fit in every course, I'd also keep embracing—not avoiding—opportunities to work alongside students in situations where neither of us have all the answers.

Meanwhile, I still laugh about how I wound up on the wrong side of the ironic twist on the construction site. My aim was for students to test the course content against the correcting influence of the world beyond the classroom, a world I subconsciously presumed to know better than they did.

But it turned out to be the teacher, not the students, who needed to be saved from his mistakes.

FURTHER RESOURCES

To learn more about how to utilize community service-learning, civic engagement, and/or community-based learning in your own courses, visit the website for Campus Compact (compact.org). The website features a Resource Library with sample syllabi from a wide range of disciplines. Among many fine books are those in the AAHE Series on Service-Learning in the Disciplines, with most books focusing on particular academic subjects.

Chapter 7

Assumptions and Acceptance in Rural Pennsylvania

Sarah Cheatle
Teacher and Podcaster, The Parenthetical Society

In January 2017, a personal decision irreversibly changed the course of one teacher's life. I was convinced that it would lead to the end of my 11-year career as a teacher, but I also recognized the necessity for my own physical and mental well-being.

Regardless of the consequences, I needed to deal with the gender dysphoria that had affected me for nearly 30 years and seek therapy. By the end of my second session, I knew I would eventually have to transition and live life full-time as Sarah. This process is difficult in the best of situations and locations, but living in rural Pennsylvania, I've heard enough racist, ethnic, and homophobic jokes to last several lifetimes.

Every bias and assumption in my brain screamed that transitioning here was not going to end well, but you know what they say about when you assume . . .

There were any number of reasons for me not to take the position in remote Pennsylvania. The district was too small, too rural, too poverty-ridden. Anything entertaining—concerts, pro sports, museums, and the like—was hours away. It was too close to home. It was too far from home. You name it, I debated it. In the end, though, this was the only job offer I received, so I packed the car and moved two days before football practice started in August 2007.

I took over as the junior high English teacher and threw myself into a number of extracurricular activities: football, track and field, quiz bowl, and too many others to remember. These activities provided the opportunity to work with students outside the classroom, but also to meet their parents.

Being a new assistant football coach in a football-crazed town meant I was a minor celebrity in the supermarket those first few months. I'm glad to say that subsided, but it also helped to forge many relationships that proved valuable in time.

As the years went on, I settled into my job and focused my curriculum on deep thought and questioning the status quo, or as much as we could in 8th grade. I developed a reputation as a rabble rouser among the faculty, both in dealing with administration and in my class. I took it upon myself to enlighten the students to the world outside our 96.5 percent White (as per the 2010 census) county.

I championed diversity of all types, be it racial, ethnic, gender, or any other minority, and I did this in part because I *knew* that they *must* come from closed-minded families, given how small our area is.

I also did this because my liberal viewpoints clashed so completely with the Republican majority here (or so I thought) that I felt it was my duty to offer a different viewpoint. We all have inherent biases and stereotypes of some sort. Most of mine are political.

By the fall of that school year, I had been going to therapy for several months and I began medical hormone treatment. My marriage of six years had ended, and I had just moved into my own apartment. It was easily a low point of my life, but it was about to get worse.

To this point, I had managed to keep things under wraps at work, but I lived with the constant fear of what would happen when I told my administration. Would I be fired? Would it become a news story? What of the town? Would something terrible happen to me?

I had read enough horror stories from the transgender community that I explicitly feared the worst. My plan had been to wait a year for hormones to do their work and then come out to everyone. The world had other plans.

Shortly after school had let out on Friday, October 6, I received a frantic phone call from a co-worker in the know. My secret was out. It was my own fault. I told someone who told someone who told many people, and that was that. I attempted to head things off, but shortly thereafter, I found myself in a meeting on short notice with administration and my union representative.

To say it went poorly would be an understatement. I had proposed emailing the faculty to brief them on the situation, but I was expressly forbidden to do this. District email was for business, and this was a personal issue. Although support was pledged, I left feeling more isolated than ever.

Several meetings followed with union leaders, as I feared for my job. Intentionally or not, my principal barely spoke to me from that day until Christmas break. I walked on eggshells, worried that each mistake would be my last in the district. Then, out of nowhere, I received support from what I believed to be the least likely source, breaking all my expectations and stereotypes.

I have already mentioned that many of my biases are political in nature. I am, in most ways, the textbook definition of "bleeding heart liberal." My principal, on the other hand, is a diehard conservative with his office television faithfully tuned to Fox News. I bristled at his daily criticisms of President Obama and cringed when he stumped for President Trump.

It seems to be part and parcel of our modern society to wear your political stripes for all to see, and yes, I, like many others, do make assumptions based on those leanings.

I expected awkwardness at best and intolerance at worst. His initial reactions filled me with dread, but then slowly, things went back to normal. We joked around again. We reconnected as co-workers as though nothing had happened.

Near the end of the school year, we discussed my plans for the fall, namely to return as Ms. Cheatle. Neither of us knew what would occur, how parents or students would react, but he promised to support me unconditionally. Unlike the meeting months prior, I believed him.

Over the summer, I entered into a PhD program in English Literature, and it seemed like the perfect time to go "full-time," so that's what I did.

My first day in the program was my first day as Sarah; either of those things alone would be enough to drive someone to tears, so doing them together was one of the best and worst decisions I ever made. I survived, though, and when I returned home in late July, I went to the school to "introduce" myself.

The principal was waiting for me, and there were definitely some awkward pauses and conversation to start, but after a few minutes, he stopped and said, "This is weird." I asked how, and he replied, "It's like I'm just talking to my friend. You look different, but you're the same person."

I laughed and said, "Of course I am; that's what I've been trying to explain to you." From then on, things were good. I don't know if his assumption was that I'd be coming to school in full drag makeup or looking like Dr. Frank-N-Furter, but there it was. Being transgender had been normalized for him. I was just his friend who happened to be transgender, and it was no longer scary.

The unknown is the true root of our fears. As much as I feared the response of the community, he feared what problems I might cause for the school. Communication, though, dissolves those fears. I posted on social media coming out as transgender, and the responses poured in. I did it for the purpose of spreading information, not praise, but the wave of kindness and support that arrived was overwhelming.

Former students, co-workers past and present, friends old and new sent words of encouragement. Perhaps most importantly, parents of current students wrote to pledge their support.

When mid-August rolled around, Ms. Cheatle prepared her lessons for the first day of school, a first day that would be completely different from any that had come before. Addressing the issue at the beginning of class led the students to be, overall, quite accepting. It wasn't good or bad; it was simply a nonissue for the majority. Only one parent emailed with concerns, but the principal politely defused the situation.

Nobody came to the school with torches or pitchforks. I was warned about one set of parents coming in for conferences, but either my appearance assuaged them, or they weren't so brave face to face because I had no issues that day. My co-workers, even those who are more conservative and may not have a rich understanding of gender identity, have been very professional, if not supportive.

The community has also continued to support me, as I still get the occasional text message of support from a parent or kind word at the store. After legally changing my name and identification, Ms. Sarah Cheatle is here to stay.

This, of course, brings us to two key follow-up questions (as any good English teacher would say): What is the moral of the story, and how can the broader education community take and apply lessons from my story to their own respective classrooms?

To answer the first question, avoid forming assumptions and stereotypes about the people in a particular community. I assumed that being largely conservative, most in my context would be intolerant of my transition, but that has absolutely not been the case. At the very least, those who are intolerant have been so in silence.

I am particularly ashamed of the assumptions I made about my principal. I should have viewed him as a friend, as a human being, but instead I transferred the perceived public perception to his individual thoughts. It is easy to do that, as over the past few decades, the transgender community has struggled to change the public narrative from negative to positive.

For too long, our characters have been depicted in television and films as deceivers or deviants, when the reality is that we are human beings that eat and breathe and have feelings like every other person. The ease with which we can slide into those beliefs is one we must fight.

As educators, we need to strive to avoid these blind spots, as unconscious bias is an inherent human trait. We might not always be able to see it in the moment, but honest self-reflection is necessary to see where our own assumptions lie.

Additionally, my situation of being transgender is one that is becoming steadily more common in our schools and society in general. Many suffer from gender dysphoria for decades without words to describe how they feel. Our students today are growing up, not only with the vocabulary to describe their experiences and feelings, but also with the support systems in place.

FURTHER RESOURCES

Educators looking to develop their awareness of transgender issues in order to better support their students, their families, and their own colleagues can search out a variety of resources that offer both generalized discussions and more education-focused treatments. Depending on your level of interest in the transgender community, you might opt for a broader overview like Julia Serano's *Whipping Girl* (2013) and Susan Stryker's *Transgender History* (2008) to give more scope to issues we face.

Meanwhile, Stephanie A. Brill and Lisa Kenney's *The Transgender Teen: A Handbook for Parents and Professionals Supporting Transgender and Non-binary Teens* and Jason Cianciotto and Sean Cahill's *LGBT Youth in America's Schools* offer a more in-depth perspective as it applies to students in high school. Other helpful texts include:

Brill, Stephanie A., and Lisa Kenney. *The Transgender Teen*. Cleis Press, 2016.
Cianciotto, Jason, and Sean Cahill. *LGBT Youth in America's Schools*. The University of Michigan Press, 2012.
Serano, Julia. *Whipping Girl: A Transsexual Woman on Sexism and the Scapegoating of Femininity*. Seal Press, 2013.
Stryker, Susan. *Transgender History: The Roots of Today's Revolution*. Seal Press, 2017.

Chapter 8

Discomfort Zone

Overcoming Ethnocentricity and Implicit Biases in Teaching

Lisa Power, PhD
Associate Professor, Saint Martin's University

Traveling to South Africa, alone, was a splurge. An invitation to present a paper at a leadership conference provided me with a reason to visit Cape Town, which was one of the first cities in the world to implement water rationing. Capetonians were to use 18 gallons per day, less than Americans normally use for a single shower.

How did people cope? How would I? Looking back, I knew that Cape Town would open my eyes to new ideas, but I did not expect that these insights would permanently change how I teach.

Travel websites featured colorful row houses found in the Bo Kaap neighborhood. The former Malay Quarter seemed to be a good place to start an adventure. Knowing little about Cape Town, and even less about Bo Kaap, I booked a room at a cozy guest house with rainwater reclamation to ease restrictions.

The social norms and cultural underpinnings that shaped me are ones of the majority communities where I have lived my whole life. As a White, over-educated college professor, I recognize that privilege allows me to travel the world with little difficulty in many ways that others cannot.

Traveling to a location in crisis, to add one more person to an overtaxed water system during a drought, felt somewhat self-serving. From the airplane window, as I looked at the ground below, I saw expensive homes with swimming pools and impoverished shanties made from corrugated metal, plywood, and plastic sheeting.

The taxi ride from the airport pushed me further into that new reality. People lived beside each other, in extreme wealth and poverty, paying no attention to each other. Neighborhoods carved by decades of racial segregation bore evidence of European luxury or developing-world squalor.

As a child, I lived in poor neighborhoods where I was often the only White child. I barely remembered those early experiences, but even in segregated Milwaukee, even the poorest houses and schools had running water and indoor plumbing.

My adult self aspires to be the traveler who savors every experience, who easily figures out a new city. Yet between the airport and my guest house, I savored nothing. Rather, I questioned my own safety and sanity for choosing to visit such a foreign place, so far from the middle-class city in America where I lived and worked.

As we turned onto the street where I would stay, we drove past a flaming pile of tires in the street. My taxi driver told me this was normal; I should not worry. Flummoxed and jetlagged, I had to ask the driver to help me sort out the fare. Rand in my wallet all looked the same. The fare cost much more than I expected. Did he rip me off? Day one and my holiday seemed like a disaster.

Culture shock feels like helplessness. Luckily, the host at my guest house helped me feel more hopeful and independent by explaining what I had experienced on the previous day: the tire fire was a common form of protest. Uber turned out to be the more affordable way to get around. Bo Kaap was a safe community, mostly inhabited by Muslims of mixed race who identify as colored or Malay Africans.

Tourists are welcome in Bo Kaap, but owners of guest houses, who are most often white South Africans, like my host, were not. The initial discomfort subsided as my assumptions were disproven, but not all at once.

Uneasy feelings and solitude had me thinking about other assumptions that I made in my life. One mistake in particular happened because of a lack of awareness of my own biases. Fortunately, the student never knew what I thought about him before I fully understood his situation; however, the mistake stayed with me, in my subconscious thought, for 15 years.

My teaching career started at a community college in the suburbs of a large, West Coast city. The late-afternoon computer applications course began in a lecture-style classroom, and we later moved to the adjoining computer lab to work on assignments.

During our first meeting, a latecomer arrived as we changed classrooms. He quietly took a seat and started working on the assignment. I introduced myself in a whisper. He asked me to call him Ibo. That night, we worked on the assignment together.

While I enjoyed meeting all of my students on that first night, the difficulty of teaching non-traditional students quickly weighed me down. Students needed individual help to complete the labs. They ran out of time, having to leave sections of the lab unfinished. It was difficult to determine who to help at length, and who to help briefly.

In retrospect, more demonstration time would have likely helped students to feel more confident working independently. I was so inexperienced, and it showed. However, I was self-conscious about something else.

In the first week, Ibo arrived late to class every evening. When he arrived, I helped him get started, which allowed him to finish on time. He left as soon as he finished, often well before other students. As a new teacher, I obsessed about what other students would think and dreaded confrontation.

Instead of talking to Ibo right away, I started to think of him as being chronically late and disrespectful. To spend more time with other students in the class, I eventually stopped providing one-on-one instruction. I wonder now: *Did I stop because I was truly busy or because I felt disrespected?*

In the second week, I asked Ibo to step outside before he left the lab. He apologized for being late and said he would accept any related consequences and shared that he grew up in Ethiopia with his family and he had much respect for teachers. His response didn't seem typical—so I thought about the situation more before saying anything else.

Ibo was sitting in his car before the next class. I noticed him, waved, and kept walking toward the classroom. Later, I casually asked why he was in his car before class, yet 20 minutes late. I expected an excuse, just not the one Ibo offered.

He told me that he was praying, and then eating; he spent the whole day, every day, fasting. I felt ashamed for knowing so little about Muslim faith. Not wanting to discriminate, I told him that I would excuse his tardiness and explain instructions to him separately again. He was appreciative. Unfortunately, I never even thought to ask what holiday he was observing.

In the late fall of 2001, Ibo likely felt reluctant to disclose his religion, as many Muslims did right after our country's terrorist attacks. After some discussion with my dean, I changed my syllabus to include a statement regarding absences for religious observances.

Years later, I came to realize that when a student is forced to disclose personal information to an untrusted teacher, learning often is compromised, regardless of the situation. I removed that statement from my syllabus, hoping instead that I would come to recognize situations like this one earlier.

Because of Ibo, I had come to terms with my own biases and how they might cause me to judge students. Ibo proved to be a good student who caught on quickly. At the end of the quarter, I felt that he should have been more upfront about his needs. My feelings were unresolved.

What if I made another similar assumption? Would I even know?

Regardless, I felt like I learned enough from the situation to move on. It turns out that there was more to learn from Ibo and that assumption.

In absentia, Ibo helped me discover a hidden weakness that has endured throughout my teaching career. Through travel, and because of Ibo, the needs of students who represent minority races and religions became more clear. After living as a minority, even for a short time, on vacation in South Africa, privilege in the context of ethnocentrism came into relief.

After two sleepless overnight flights, crossing three continents, I slept for much of my first day in Cape Town. As the sun disappeared on my first African day, I woke to an Islamic call to prayer—a hymn that I would hear three times daily during my stay. Each time, I paused to thank God for my beautiful life. The haunting and sacred prayers of a muezzin will stay with me forever, even though I have practiced Christianity for my whole life.

Jetlag subsided on day two, just when hunger set in. I ventured out into Bo Kaap, mostly to find food and water. My guest house was located beside Auwal Mosque, the first mosque built in South Africa, in 1794. After a few minutes outside, I realized that I looked entirely out of place with pale, White skin and blond hair pulled back into a bun. Even my sneakers seemed wrong.

My phone and wallet seemed vulnerable. I tucked them deeper into my backpack. Feeling targeted and afraid of Muslims with black and brown skin, I bravely wandered downtown to the tourist attractions. The Protestant cathedral where Archbishop Desmond Tutu once preached sheltered me from swarms of panhandlers and street children. Bathing in the light of stained-glass windows and the smell of old hymnals, I settled down. *Here I am safe.*

Around lunchtime, I finally found a grocery store. Anxiety set in again when I realized that I was the only White person in the crowded market. Women wearing hijab, headwraps or hats; drab dresses or tunics or bright dashiki shirts. Men in suits with Madiba shirts or tracksuits. Hurriedly, I found food and bottled water, hoping that no one would notice me. Waiting in line, I heard the banter of a young couple.

She smiled and grabbed his watch, "How much longer? I'm so hungry."

"Only four more hours, love. But then I have to get to work."

The way he spoke and dressed reminded me of Ibo, who I had not seen or thought of in many years. Over the course of my teaching career, I learned about Muslim traditions, so I knew that during Ramadan, Muslims endured extreme hunger during the day.

Here I was, standing in line, hungry, like all the other people in the store. Maybe they were hungry because of fasting. Maybe they just needed groceries. I was hungry in a jetlag kind of way; simultaneously hungry and disoriented. For no reason other than proximity, I felt connected to these strangers in hunger. They would not eat until 5:00 pm, so I decided to do the same.

Walking back to my room, I passed a mosque where men stood outside, listening to an Imam preaching through a megaphone. The message was about acceptance and appreciation of the hunger that Allah has given us. *Okay God, I'm listening.* Islam and Christianity are more similar than different.

A White woman, standing alone, wearing casual travel clothing and no hijab cannot blend in. But I did; not a single person objected to my presence. My American socialization and beliefs led me to believe that someone might.

As I stood peacefully and contemplated God's love, American conditioning pushed me to subconsciously, and needlessly, fear Muslims. I chose acceptance and found opportunities to open myself to the beauty of a new culture. While I was in South Africa, I reflected on my blind spots. What would make me fear people Muslims or people with black or brown skin?

In my time in South Africa, I wrestled with what shaped me. Did the entertainment industry criminalize Blackness, or has it ended up that way because audiences already believe that Black men are criminals? Have we excluded Islamic people and stories from our culture because the news media and entertainment industry connected Islam to ongoing terror threats? There were many influences upon my assumptions that were becoming clear.

By the time my son and husband joined me for the last week of my trip, I felt comfortable engaging in conversations with South Africans. People who were oppressed under apartheid told stories that helped us understand history, culture, and forgiveness. They were particularly kind when they learned they were speaking to a teacher.

My son, born with so much privilege, as they said, felt loved by South African people. I pictured myself telling my friends back home about meeting elephants, giraffes, and penguins in the wild, or about hiking at the edge of a continent. But the stories I tell most often, return me to the spirit of people who have been freed from oppression.

A person's race, gender, nationality, and faith shape how they experience reality. In South Africa, where less than 10 percent of the population is White, I was a minority. In Bo Kaap, where Islam first came to South Africa, I prayed as a Lutheran. My modest teacher's salary offered me enough financial security to travel, which is a blessing. Privilege allows for freedom to worship, speak openly, and love whomever I want. An education allows me to serve others. These are gifts.

Yet as I stood as the only White person in a grocery store, and in front of the mosque, I had to confront subconscious biases that controlled my emotions. I was not in danger. People were not targeting me. After I reconciled my own implicit biases, I realized that I was as safe as I would be in America. I'm sure I stood out, but I constantly reminded myself that these differences really only mattered to me. *South Africans saw my differences, and theirs, as gifts that we give to each other.*

Traveling across land and oceans to return home, I reconciled all that I learned. Witnessing Muslim traditions became beautiful and sacred. Fasting is difficult and admirable. Standing out as a White person can be lonely and frightening. My own tendencies were undeniable in these contexts. Clearly, I was blind to biases in my teaching.

As teachers, we have to know what shapes us, so that we can relate to students who may not seem to be like us. In choosing to see our differences as gifts, trust and respect might follow. When my family was welcomed into a beautiful Zulu community, we felt love. No longer strangers in a foreign land, we felt ready to learn about a new place and culture. Our job as teachers is to create a community of love, where students feel welcomed and accepted for all the gifts they bring.

Teachers create inclusive communities by paying attention to their own biases and beliefs. Ethnocentrism happens when educators, curriculum designers, and administrators favor, or rely exclusively on, their own experiences and values. Those of us raised and educated within a Western European context tend to impose our own beliefs and values on others, perhaps without even realizing that we do. Rather than taking the initiative to learn about the unique cultural traditions of others, people in majority groups often expect others to educate them on their traditions.

We strengthen our collective identity and reduce ethnocentrism when we reflect upon the differences between ourselves and others. When students from minority groups feel welcomed into an inclusive classroom, they arrive with greater capacity for learning. What can teachers do to assure that this happens?

Each of us relies on an unconscious set of attitudes and beliefs as we make decisions and behave in certain ways. For example, you might sense the need to stop walking when you reach the crosswalk of a busy street, where you might not even slow down on side streets. Why?

Years of pedestrian experience guides your subconscious thought: a busy street presents more danger than a side street. Our brains create shortcuts, to help us reduce the amount of data we need to keep track of, especially when we are multitasking. Outside of the conscious thought process, our brains create associations from the information it takes in. In some cases, these associations turn into generalizations.

When teaching, our brains create generalizations, also called implicit biases. Years of experience train teachers to know how to spot cheating on a test, or when to push for a deeper response in a class discussion. Socialization trains us to intuitively think and act in the ways that we do. Without even realizing that we teach and respond from our own reference frames, we dismiss, assume, correct, and share. Moving outside our comfort zones teaches us to remember the differences between ourselves and our peers.

Everyone holds implicit biases. Implicit biases lead us to favor people from groups like our own. When students experience the opposite end of favoritism, whether intentional or not, they can develop negative implicit biases about the groups they identify with.

Teachers can reduce the effect these biases have on our actions. Teachers who learn to recognize stereotypes can respond differently when they encounter situations where implicit bias might influence behavior. Teachers who work to reduce ethnocentrism may find it easier to relate to a student's point of view. Students feel more confident and more welcomed into a learning environment when they can relate to their teachers.

To reduce ethnocentrism in education, explore other cultures using websites, picture books, photos, and videos. Let curiosity drive your learning. Meet with ambassadors, including cultural and community leaders. Explore neighborhoods where you can observe and learn to respect different traditions. Shop at a store where you will be a minority. Ask a religious leader or teacher to explain cultural traditions or attend a worship service for a faith that is very different from your own.

Discomfort helps us to become aware of our differences, so that we can recognize our biases when we engage with others.

In these moments when you are the only person like you, think about how you feel being a minority, even if that feeling is temporary. How would learning be different for you, if you felt that way in a classroom? Consider factors that might contribute to how a person of a minority group might act when questioned about behavior or beliefs. Then resolve to act in ways that would help people of all backgrounds and traditions to feel like their differences are appreciated and important.

As you engage with new cultures and people, think about how your culture aligns or contrasts with these new experiences. Finally, reflect on how you can bring what you have learned and experienced into your classroom, your teaching practices, your curriculum, and your daily life.

FURTHER RESOURCES

Teachers interested in developing cultural competence when it comes to religion would be best served by learning about a variety of religions and their beliefs and traditions.

Global Voices and Global Visions: Education for Excellence, Understanding, Peace and Sustainability by Betsy Gunzelmann provides an overview of the obstacles students face in trying to access education (including safety concerns) in our modern world where ideologies clash, and touts a globally informed approach to education that can shift our thinking about how our worldviews are shaped by our environment and how we can approach teaching in a way that promotes understanding and peace in spite of that fact.

Part III

FOSTERING RELATIONSHIPS AND ADVOCATING FOR STUDENTS

Chapter 9

Be a Voice for the Voiceless

Beth Jarzabek
Middle School Teacher

I got my first teaching job at the age of 23, after spending the entire summer searching for a position with no luck. I was fresh out of college with little experience in a time when there was a glut of highly qualified elementary educators flooding the job market. In a strange turn of events which somehow involved my mother unintentionally impersonating me on the telephone with the Diocesan office, a local Catholic school gained a new fourth-grade teacher, two weeks before school started.

I knew nothing about this school and its procedures and policies. As is often the case with "newbie" teachers, my fourth-grade counterpart took me under her wing and taught me the basics—teacher "duties," dismissal procedures, staff meeting schedules, and the like. Taking copious notes, I soaked up all of the minutiae that makes up the day-to-day routine of an elementary school classroom.

During one of these informational sessions, the school's Enrichment Program, which provided a small group of high achieving students an opportunity a few times a week to enhance their learning with a project-based class, was discussed. As my mentor sat and explained this program, she scrutinized the list of proposed students.

"We need to cut some of these kids. This class should be smaller," she told me.

Because she had been at the school for several years and knew these students, I deferred to her expertise. Though I didn't see it at the time, as I look back now, I can see her cuts were random—and all from my class list.

When the first day of school arrived, I was overjoyed to find that the son of one of my former (and favorite) teachers was placed in my classroom. As excited as I was to have him in my class, I was nervous to live up to the example that his mother had set as an educator. Imagine my dismay when I realized that his name was one of those who had been cut from the Enrichment Program.

Imagine my further distress when I received a message on my home answering machine on the third day of school when the list of the selected students was released. Always the consummate professional and kind soul, my former teacher didn't attack me in my inexperience, but rather asked the questions that any parent in her position would ask—questions that I myself as an educator should have asked.

"What are the criteria for the Enrichment program?"
"Was there something that changed in my son's performance last year
    that would cause his exclusion from the program this year?"
"What is the class size limit? Why are only that number of students allowed?"
And finally,
"Would you reconsider putting my son in the program?"

As you can probably imagine, I stumbled and fumbled my way through that conversation. I didn't have the answers that she was looking for and I was honest with her. I told her I had assumed that my mentor teacher knew the students and the school better than I did and allowed her to make my class decisions for me.

Apologizing, I promised to do what I had failed to do before the start of the year—go in the very next day and advocate for her son to retain his spot in the program.

And I did.

The next day I went in early to talk to my counterpart. I rehearsed what I was going to say in the car, garnering the courage to speak up to this veteran teacher and preparing myself to stand my ground. Practicing arguments and counter-arguments, I felt exhausted by the time I pulled into the parking lot. It was time to fight for this student and his right to be included in the program.

Walking into my mentor's classroom, I took a deep breath, and stated my case without stopping to take a single breath through my entire speech. As I finished I steeled myself for the confrontation sure to follow.

But it didn't.

Instead she shrugged and said, "Sure. If you think he should be in the program, put him on the list."

And that was the end of it.

This demonstrates the importance of the teacher voice as an advocate for students and how vital it is to employ. It was made clear that the decision to remove the student from that program was not only not in his best interest but also arbitrary. The fact that his mother advocated to me for what was best for him, which in turn pushed me to do the same to my colleague may have changed the course of this student's year in fourth grade.

Being removed from that program through no fault of his own may have damaged his confidence and how he looked at the school experience going forward.

It most certainly changed my teaching career.

This year marks my seventeenth year of teaching and I would like to think that my voice when it comes to advocating for my students has gotten louder and stronger. This past year, I had the opportunity to pilot our new Genius Hour elective. This class is largely student directed, project-based learning which requires students to pick a passion project to research, complete, and present.

When trying to decide the criteria for entrance into this class, the seventh grade English teachers decided that they would make their own lists of their current students whom they thought deserved to be put into a class called "Genius Hour." After going through their rosters and analyzing the names through a criterion known only to themselves, they gave their list of finalists to the Guidance Department. Twelve kids. All Honors students. No Individualized Education Plans. No behavior issues. Twelve kids to be split between two semesters.

Naturally, I was livid, not only because these colleagues were supposed to make this decision for me, but more because they excluded a huge number of kids because they weren't the ideal students in their minds.

I would like to say that I walked calmly to the Guidance Department to express my displeasure, but I think storming the office might be a more accurate description. As our very quiet and mild-mannered guidance counselor came to his door, I (more forcibly than I truly meant to) blurted out "Just give me all the kids!"

He abided by my wishes and any student who wanted to take that elective was allowed to. Not surprisingly, some of the best projects that were created during those Genius Hours were made by those very kids who would have been excluded from the course given the guidelines set forth at the onset.

The moral of these stories is simple: Use your "teacher voice." Advocate for the children in your charge. Speak up for your profession. Make yourself heard. This doesn't mean you have to be the loudest or the most aggressive person in the room; this means that you need to find an effective way to get your point across and do what is right for your kids.

In order to bolster your confidence to employ your voice as a teacher to advocate for students, carry out research on the issue or topic at hand and enter conversations with a solid understanding of the salient points. This may be knowing the criteria for certain in-school programs, the benefits of a program you want, or both sides of a parent issue.

You might also collect data and evidence. While data can be a loaded term, often used by administration to show how we have once again not reached Adequate Yearly Progress on our annual state-mandated standardized testing, as a teacher advocate, you should collect, analyze, and use your own data to strengthen your argument.

Teacher-collected evidence is a powerful tool, especially when it provides a face and story to a student who may be pigeon-holed by their test scores, background, or behavior.

Finally, be persistent. In advocating for something that you feel passionately about, you must never accept "no." If your colleagues shut down an idea that you truly feel will help your students, try another approach. If administration is initially resistant to a pilot program that you feel passionate about, present your research and make a strong case. If you feel a student is not receiving the services that he or she needs, gather your evidence and push for the accommodations that your student needs to succeed.

As educators, we are not given six figure salaries, company cars, and extensive benefit packages. What we are given is the power to make a difference in the lives of the children who are placed in our care. And with this power comes immense responsibility.

The responsibility to make sure that our students are able to reach their full potential. The responsibility to ensure that each of our students feels safe and included. The responsibility to strengthen the foundation beneath each student as they make their way through their educational career. In order to fulfill all of these obligations, you must use your "teacher voice." Make yourself heard.

FURTHER RESOURCES

Teachers interested in both information and inspiration in regards to becoming an advocate for their students can also read the Education World article, "Be a Student Advocate—Top Nine Tips. (https://www.educationworld.com /a_admin/top-ways-to-advocate-for-students.shtml)

While this article is based upon a guide for administrators, *The Principal as Student Advocate: A Guide for Doing What Is Best for All Students*, the practical tips provided also apply to those educators who choose to lead without leaving their classrooms.

Another amazing resource is "Fighting the Good Fight: How to Advocate for Your Students Without Losing Your Job" (https://www.readingrockets .org/article/fighting-good-fight-how-advocate-your-students-without-losing -your-job) by Rick Lavoie. This extensive piece gives insight into common "behind the scenes" issues and "players" that often clash with the efforts of advocates. Going beyond general tips, the article provides a plethora of specific suggestions, possible scenarios, and constructive tactics in the fight for what is best for students.

Chapter 10

Learning to Fly

Why Developing Student Voice Matters

Jane Saunders, PhD
Associate Professor, Literacy
Texas State University

When I started as an English teacher in 1992, my greatest aspiration was to instill in students that their words mattered and to help develop them as thinkers and doers. We had an expansive curriculum, a compelling selection of novels for literature circles, and a principal who trusted his teachers.

Classroom discussions were a mélange of a variety of perspectives and experiences through film, novels, and songs. We contemplated the plight of humans to enact a meaningful life while paying the bills. Getting the kids to school. Making a contribution to the world. As the students were asked to consider their purpose, they wrote passionately about seeking work that could sustain their interest, opportunities to help others, a life that had meaning and that offered freedom and fun.

Things went along swimmingly until testing season came when everything had to be put aside to work on persuasive writing, required on state assessments in Texas. This was still the early days of standardized testing, when the test was viewed as more of a nuisance than an outright threat. These students hailed from middle-class suburban homes and received high marks, so the shadow side of such a mandate never felt all that menacing.

Years later, after moving into a large urban district, terms like *adequate yearly progress* and the need to increase test performance regardless of its potential negative impact on actual student learning became de rigueur.

The shadow arrived in the form of curriculum guides, worksheets, and mind-numbingly dull informational passages all directed at leveraging greater success on state-mandated tests.

I thought to myself, "How is it possible legislators think this is good for students?" My students were visibly bored and disengaged as I managed to follow the script briefly to survive evaluations.

Learning centers afforded a different approach to teaching from many of my secondary colleagues as a key component of my pedagogical practice. This allowed students to take charge of their learning and positioned the teacher as a facilitator, lessening the need for direct teaching.

For example, students engaged in mystery centers to explore character and plot. Activities included listening and responding to audio recordings of short stories with plot twists; engaging with an interactive CD to solve a crime; playing the board game Clue; and using textual evidence to collect data on potential culprits of modern mysteries.

Through learning centers, students investigated the Holocaust by looking at the art and written work of children; assessing tone by drawing charcoal images of events described in *Night* by Elie Wiesel; and reviewing primary source documents like train schedules, memos to key figures in the United States, or other artifacts from World War II.

Employing centers demonstrated that students could become engrossed in literacy when given meaningful opportunities to enact reading, writing, speaking, and listening. The next logical step was to build a bridge between these learning centers and life. I began to wonder, "How do I take the strong opinions and ideas surfacing from center activity and harness these for good? Is there even a space for student voices in the current educational realm?"

This shift altered my thinking as I began placing students' lived experiences and connections front and center in my planning.

Students want to tell their story—even the quiet ones. Yet in our flurry of curriculum coverage or worry over time, we often forget the simplest of truths. Manifesting all around us are technological tools, tablets, and social media offering spaces for students to develop, curate, and author their identities. Yet in a crowded school day that privileges informational reading and writing over personal expression, students learn to write in a voice that is neutral, false, and often dull.

While research tells us that new learning is shaped by experience and background knowledge, schools often limit opportunities for students to say, "This is what I believe; and, here is how I've come to take this stance." This is particularly true in grade-level classrooms, where students might benefit most from confronting multiple perspectives through respectful dialogue.

These are necessary skills for success in life after high school and in participating constructively in civic life. Barred from opportunities to speak up in school, students reach outward to have their voices heard.

Pew research on social media from 2018 suggests that 88% of young people—aged 18 to 24—use social platforms like YouTube, Facebook, Snapchat, and Instagram. This number shrinks as those participating in the Pew study age, suggesting younger students plug into social media more than the prior millennial generation. They draw on these tools in unexpected ways, too.

For example, an article in *The Atlantic* titled "Teens are Debating the News on Instagram" suggests not only that young people are reading the news but that many have created "flop accounts" [defined as "fail" accounts] to have unfiltered, less public conversations about things they find objectionable, like a YouTuber's racism, homophobia, or to disseminate "cringeworthy content for entertainment purposes." They are engaging actively in the skills sought in state-mandated tests, but in much deeper ways than is often possible in those very measurements.

Students are well-versed in blending writing, social networking, and argumentation skills and delivering those publicly. This was the case when a group of student journalists critiqued a school speaker they believed was pitching a dangerous message to their community.

They penned an editorial that was disseminated in the school's news magazine online and through print. After the speaker clapped back via Twitter and his company blog, a public debate ensued through Twitter and Reddit, culminating in state, national, and international news coverage. Student voices were definitely heard, and they carried with them this learning experience as they left for college.

We are witnessing a burgeoning response among students to social issues, politics, and the way these intersect with their lived experiences. Examples abound, like the widespread response to gun violence in the wake of the Parkland High School shootings in 2018, walkouts on campus related to the

"Me, Too" or "Black Lives Matter" movement, and public meetings with legislators related to school funding.

However, it is more rare to see teachers leveraging student engagement as a bridge into content. This is understandable; schools worry about public critique if they allow students or teachers to take a stand. And, given that standardized tests offer minimal opportunities for students to voice their learning in authentic ways, schools likely see no benefit to developing student voice.

So, given these limitations on teachers' pedagogical practice, how might they engage in meaningful conversations that foment opportunities for students to speak to their experiences? Contrary to how teaching is portrayed in the media, there are large portions of time distributed throughout a school day when formal teaching is not occurring. Teachers get to school early, have passing periods, lunch, or planning time. They participate in assemblies, pep rallies, or extracurricular events.

In addition, there are moments in the classroom where interactions between teacher and student are co-constructed, less formal, and often more meaningful for learning. The research community calls this *third space*, the space between home and school where authentic and informal interactions can occur. This is visible among teachers who sponsor clubs, coach sports and academic teams, or stay late to tutor or serve duty at the bus line. There is a great deal of informal learning taking place around the edges of the school day.

These third spaces are also where students talk about their challenges, tell their stories, and where teachers can commiserate with them when they fall. These connections along the margins of the school day serve as opportunities for students to contemplate and respond to their world in a safe space. And they have a sneaky way of reappearing in a different form in the classroom.

As our classrooms increase in linguistic, racial, and cultural diversity, the importance of nurturing *confianza*—defined as mutual trust and reciprocity—among students and families has come into sharp relief. When teachers partner with parents and their local community to help bridge home knowledge to the school curriculum, students feel respected and honored. They also see the connection between what they are learning in school and what they are seeing in the larger world.

Teaching is an intentional act that requires educators and students to negotiate multiple spheres of life—school, home, electronic—all within the context of an assigned curriculum. It is within this realm that students begin to make connections among disparate spaces and to understand that learning is not just an in-school behavior, it is necessary for growth and success throughout our lives.

As such, it is a teacher's responsibility to help students discover their voices as intellectually curious beings because at the end of the day, we are not just preparing students to do well in our respective grade level or content courses.

It is a teacher's responsibility to bolster students not just with knowledge gleaned from a well-constructed and viable curriculum. They must also send students on their way with the capacity to respond to their world in a measured and cogent manner obtained through practice, through engagement with others with differing perspectives, and through the opportunity to change one's mind.

Teachers begin this process by developing student voices so that they will have the requisite skills to grow and thrive, participate actively in their collective community, and find meaningful ways to contribute to the world. As teachers, when we help students develop their voices, we are nudging their intellect to safely leave the nest. We are preparing them to flourish, to fledge—to develop their wings for future flight.

FURTHER RESOURCES

There are a variety of related resources to help novice teachers expand their repertoire online. For example, NCTE's www.readwritethink.org hosts a searchable database for creative teaching ideas related to literacy.

Rethinking Schools https://www.rethinkingschools.org/ and *Teaching Tolerance* https://www.tolerance.org/classroom-resources/teaching-strategies offer innovative ways to help students engage in thinking and writing about their lived experiences, their community, and the world they will one day inherit. These resources relate to current events and help teachers connect to course content in language arts, social studies, and science classes.

In service to the development of voice, I have begun showing digital shorts that represent a wide swath of story and experience to my undergraduate students, studying to become teachers. There are a wealth of good options at websites like Soul Pancake [http://soulpancake.com/] and StoryCorps [https://storycorps.org/] that provide a variety of perspectives and generate active conversations upon viewing.

I recently asked students to make connections between a Tyler Merritt video produced by "Now This" called "Before You Call the Cops" [http://newsvideo.su/video/8866102] and an animation about Ron McNair, one of the first African-American astronauts, who died in the space shuttle Challenger explosion in 1986 [https://storycorps.org/animation/eyes-on-the-stars/].

In the latter video, McNair's brother discusses how the police were called to intervene in their small South Carolina town when Ron, aged 9 at the time, asked to check out books from the public library serving the white community.

This anecdote is used as an example of McNair's persistence and commitment to learning, but viewed through the lens of Black Lives Matter and the repeated documentation of white citizens calling the police on community members of color, students began telling their own related stories of unequal treatment, uneasiness when they did not speak up, and concerns about their future students. These perspectives matter, and it is up to teachers to open up the space for such stories to surface.

Chapter 11

Learning from the Nuts and Bolts

Listening to Yourself and Your Learners

Katherine Baker, EdD
Assistant Professor of Education
Elon University

I moved to North Carolina from Michigan when I was 23 and started teaching fifth grade at a rural, Title One elementary school. Previous to this, I had completed student teaching and one year as an elementary mathematics interventionist in a Michigan public school system.

Teaching that first year in North Carolina meant learning how to navigate being an outsider to the school, district, and even state. It meant learning to build and establish trust with the school community, and humbly accepting again and again that trust was not a given. It meant constantly reevaluating who I wanted to be as a teacher in that space.

What is often overlooked in our profession is that when entering the field in our early twenties, teachers are simultaneously figuring out their own identities outside of the classroom. They are still sorting out personal beliefs around politics, religion, friendships, and wellness, and all of those belief structures would have grand implications on who they will be as teachers.

During the induction year, teachers would benefit greatly from dedicating time to reflecting upon their personal beliefs and how those beliefs shape their professional beliefs and how they show up in the classroom. But so often teachers neglect the time for deep reflection, sacrificing it instead to the hustle and overwhelming obligations of the career.

We adopt the survival technique of listening to every other teacher within proximity about who we should be and how we should teach.

While our profession depends on learning from others, thriving from this learning comes when we are thoughtful and reflective about the advice and knowledge offered. In my early 20s, I was latching on to others' practices and enacting their teaching beliefs and pedagogies without contextual insight or critique.

Enter the nuts and bolts of teaching.

During my own induction year, our school custodian would check on me throughout my late afternoon and evening planning sessions. For the third week in a row, he was replacing a missing bolt on a tilting desk leg.

"I can't believe another bolt went missing from a desk," I said to him while grading.

"Yeah, the students really like to turn them and probably like the distraction a lost bolt causes."

I stopped and looked up at him. I was embarrassed that I had not caught on sooner.

Of course someone was turning the bolt on the desk and taking it out. It takes a human hand to remove a nut and bolt. I had naively assumed (or perhaps it was denial) that the bolts were simply falling out and rolling away because the desks were old.

I flashed back to every classroom moment when a desk started to tilt and its contents spewed out on the floor. It was always mid-lesson, it was always when attention was wanted, and it was always when I was so consumed with the act of my teaching 'show' that I was not thinking about who that teaching was for.

My students were begging me to get to know them, to observe them, to listen to them; I was too busy replicating every other teacher and trying to nail perfect implementation of their lessons or advice.

I had entered the profession with some background work in a paradigm known as Cognitively Guided Instruction (CGI)[1] and used this to guide my mathematics teaching. CGI is grounded in how teachers use knowledge about children's thinking and problem-solving to make decisions as they plan and implement mathematics instruction.

That induction year, I was continuing my learning around CGI with ongoing professional development offered by a local university professor. Drawing on CGI, I was focused on children's thinking and eliciting their mathematical ideas to integrate into my mathematics teaching.

It was not a coincidence that a desk crisis with a missing bolt never occurred during my mathematics block. Thanks to an insightful comment from our custodian, I came to recognize my stunted vision of CGI. Why wasn't I taking that same belief around listening to and valuing student thinking and applying it across the school day? If I cared about children's mathematical ideas, shouldn't I also care about their ideas across all subjects?

And shouldn't I be showing them that I care about their ideas and who they were outside of academic moments?

Teaching was and is more than a show; it has to be flexible enough to revolve around learners. But opening up the whole day to listening to students and learning with them instead of teaching *at* them would take courage and vulnerability. To enact student-centered pedagogical approaches, teachers must deviate from such style shows and learn how to steer the in-the-moment discussions toward learning goals.

While there was not a miraculous turnaround in my teaching the very next day after the bolt revelation, there was an awareness and an openness. There was also a commitment to major changes going into the following year around community-building and classroom structures.

Instead of accepting a "turn your card to red" behavior system because that's what others used, I began to think about the management structures needed for a classroom that was focused on student thinking and student involvement. If I was going to stay in the profession, I had to take time to reflect on my personal and professional beliefs and dig deep into who I wanted to be in the classroom for the sake of the learners. Teachers needs this time to reflect.

This is especially true of our preservice and early-career teachers, especially when undergoing early observations of teaching. A personal motto in approaching coaching of preservice teachers is to offer "space and grace." This motto roots from an understanding that preservice teachers need space and grace from their supervisors and instructors to figure teaching out; in return, preservice teachers must give those same supervisors and instructors the space and grace to figure out ways to best support them in doing that work.

As a teaching profession, we often overlook giving new teachers the space and grace to explore and stumble. Humans in their early twenties are charged with facilitating learning and development over rooms of other humans, yet are still navigating their own development.

Often my manners of support are grounded in my comfort area of mathematics and CGI. CGI is used as an entryway for listening to children's thinking. The second edition *Children's Mathematics: Cognitively Guided Instruction* book[2] shares typical mathematical strategies, applicable teaching strategies, and companion videos of children and teachers interacting around mathematical ideas. This text and its videos serve as models of teaching practices that welcome learners' contributions into the classroom space.

This text and philosophical view also offers a hook into the beauty of listening to children within one content area, with the hopes that preservice and beginning teachers will then become interested in learning about children's thinking holistically. Then, if they become overwhelmed with advice overload in their own teaching careers, they may come back to the solid ground of CGI and the importance of integrating children's thinking into the day.

Alternatively, beginning teachers may find grounding in whatever their personal CGI is. If children's mathematical thinking is not the launching pad for integrating learners' voices and bringing teaching joy, perhaps other teachers will take stock in listening to children through literacy instruction, or through the lens of Responsive Classrooms, or through culturally sustaining pedagogies (see Further Resources section below).

CGI was just the beginning of a pathway to learning how to listen to students and letting their needs, interests, and lives take the lead. A piece of overarching advice for beginning teachers is to find the thing that makes you a teacher who honors yourself and all the learners in your space, manifest that daily, and let it push your professional growth.

Even as later-career teachers, personal beliefs still evolve as lived experiences change, but confidence around who we are and what we stand for is much more settled than it may be at 22 or 23 years old, when we often enter the profession. It is important to take a critical lens to what one hears and sees in the teaching world, and to also open one's self to being critical and reflective about their own teaching practices.

A colleague reflected on the end of his second year of teaching: "We are imperfect adults, teaching imperfect children, imperfectly." We all need to give each other and ourselves some space and grace to figure it out and find our CGI. Oh, and we need to look out for the runaway bolts, because they signal a transformation is on the horizon.

FURTHER RESOURCES

Teachers, teacher educators, and educational supporters who want to learn more about teaching mathematics that elicits and honors students' thinking can start by familiarizing themselves with the National Council of Teachers of Mathematics (NCTM, https://www.nctm.org/) and the organization's *Principles to Actions: Ensuring Mathematical Success for All* and its position statement on Access and Equity in Mathematics Education (https://www.nctm.org/Standards-and-Positions/Position-Statements/Access-and-Equity-in-Mathematics-Education/).

As mentioned, Carpenter and colleagues' second edition of *Children's Mathematics: Cognitively Guided Instruction* also provides video exemplars and resources for how one might facilitate student-driven mathematics instruction.

For information on Responsive Classroom, see https://www.responsive-classroom.org/, and for information on Culturally Sustaining Pedagogies, see Paris, D., & Alim, H. S. (Eds.). (2017). *Culturally Sustaining Pedagogies: Teaching and Learning for Justice in a Changing World.* Teachers College Press.

NOTES

1. Carpenter, T. P., Fennema, E., Franke, M. L., Levi, L., & Empson, S. B. (1999). *Children's Mathematics: Cognitively Guided Instruction* (1st ed.). Portsmouth, NH: Heinemann.

   Carpenter, T. P., Fennema, E., Franke, M. L., Levi, L., & Empson, S. B. (2014). *Children's Mathematics: Cognitively Guided Instruction* (2nd ed.). Portsmouth, NH: Heinemann.

2. Carpenter, Fennema, Franke, Levi, and Empson (2014).

Chapter 12

Safe Havens, Love, and Connection

Learning to Co-teach Effectively

Darius Montez Phelps

Pre-K Specialist, Georgia Department
of Early Care and Learning

When I became an educator and then a lead infant teacher with my own class-room, it appeared that I had it all together.

Looking back, people commended me on all the good I had accomplished that year—from receiving the Georgia Association for the Education of Young Children "Child Caregiver of the Year" Award, to presenting a TEDx-UGA talk, being nominated for an NAACP Image Award, to finishing my master's degree in less than a year. Yet, few knew about the personal, emotional struggles I faced (and continue to face) along this path as I struggled with confidence, questioning my every decision related to my teaching.

I constantly worried if my best was enough and if I was doing all that I possibly could for the little ones in my care.

My highest goal as an educator is and always will be to create a safe haven for my students and fellow educators, where they are free to explore, and, most importantly, to be their true selves without an ounce of judgement. We are all in this together, as a family and community. While it's a straight-forward goal that's simple to articulate, it's one that is much more difficult to execute while negotiating the daily challenges one faces as a classroom teacher.

Going into my second year as the Lead Infant Teacher with infant-aged children, nothing had changed about who I was or how I approached my teaching, but I felt an unfamiliar disconnect within the walls of my classroom. It is my belief that for our students to feel safe, they need to have a loving environment in which to learn, grow, and thrive. They also need to feel a bond with their teachers.

This particular school year, though, the students in my charge were older and had dominant and strong personalities. Having such a different classroom make-up served as a challenge, but one that I looked forward to tackling everyday nonetheless.

I had come to accept that this year would be more of a challenge and I readied myself to grow and change to meet the issues arising from a new sort of class composition head-on. And yet, I could not shake the feeling that something was off in the classroom.

Whenever things go wrong, I typically and instinctively look inward first, questioning my assumptions and interrogating my feelings to see if I am the source of the divide. Yet, no matter how much meditating and self-reflection I did, I kept coming to the conclusion that the problem was bigger than myself. After all, like each previous year, I would come to work each day, feeling confident in my abilities and what my students could do.

I shifted my focus to my assistant. My assistant was the complete opposite of me as a teacher and as a person. While we were the same age and she was hired at the same time as I began to work full time, she had less experience working with children at any age and often relied more on "research-based practices" instead of trusting her own intuition and ability to identify and modify the appropriate teaching practices each child needed.

My approach, on the other hand, was more heart-based and centered on human connection. As we taught together, this gulf in our approaches had grown into a sizable problem.

As the teaching year progressed, I clung even harder to my principles. From my perspective, as a teacher, there comes a time where one must consider the research base while also doing what feels right from the heart when it comes to the well-being of your students. Given the tender age of these little ones, early childhood teachers often bond with them like parents even if you aren't a parent yourself. And what I observed in the classroom seemed to underscore my beliefs and approach.

Even halfway through the year, when everyone was well-acquainted, my students were still not bonding with my assistant. Instead, just as it had been at the start of the school year, all eight students seemed to prefer me, clinging to me as soon as they entered the classroom each morning.

Their desire to be close to me was inspiring yet also overwhelming, espe-cially since we had intentionally attempted to support the children's healthy bonding process with *both* of us since the beginning of the school year. I knew it was important that the students were able to bond with my assistant, too, since she played a significant role in the classroom and their learning process as well.

At this point, I felt myself on the verge of a breakdown even though I knew I couldn't give in and let myself be consumed by negativity. I stand firm in believing that leadership is something that is demonstrated, not announced, and that is the approach I took with working alongside my assistant, in spite of our growing divide.

For the remainder of the year, I did all that I could to put the needs of my children and my assistant before mine. I was at their beck and call constantly, and the more I gave them, the less time I spent taking care of myself.

Looking back, I can see just how deleterious this was, not only for my own well-being but also for that of my assistant and students. The classroom is not just a place of comfort and solace for students. Teachers also need to feel safe there, recognizing that there is no challenge that cannot be understood and conquered. This is how we truly are able to be all that we can for our students, by being there first and foremost, for ourselves—but I didn't realize that until much later.

I wish I would have addressed the issues with an open, respectful, and heartfelt conversation. During that school year, I had gotten so immersed in the drama and confusion I identified as radiating from my assistant that it had begun to affect the place that was supposed to serve as a safe haven for us all.

I was focused on what I perceived to be my assistant's lack of passion, enthusiasm, and love for the children and I let that affect my confidence and self-esteem. At the end of the year, I felt like I had been beaten, bruised, bro-ken, and most importantly burned out.

It wasn't until later that I learned how to work effectively with a co-teacher. If I had another shot at that school year, I would have sought to come from the same place of love and connection that I relied on in interacting with my stu-dents. Co-teaching is challenging, but with an open and connected approach, it can be enriching for everyone, because there are double the resources and relationships in the classroom with two teachers.

Yet, I hadn't been prepared in my formal training to approach and handle a breakdown in the co-teaching relationship. So little support and direction around how to develop a strong co-teaching partnership was afforded to me, and I was thereby privy to the pitfalls.

Through reflection, I've come to recognize the need that year for the following:

1. Communication and conflict resolution skills.

   Had I felt confident in my ability to communicate my observations and perspective to my assistant, I likely would have had a much different experience that school year. While it is clear our teaching philosophies were much different, a difficult conversation could have helped us bridge that divide.

   Perhaps in lesson planning, she could contribute research-based strategies, and in the execution of the lessons, I could demonstrate my caring for students, living out the ethos of the importance of a safe haven to support their learning. What a gift clear and open communication would have been for everyone. After all, I'm sure my teaching assistant had differing expectations around how things would go in that classroom, just as I did!

2. Addressing the power imbalance.

   In my co-teaching relationship, I was the lead teacher and my assistant was, well, my assistant. An honest and open conversation about the power imbalance inherent to such a setup might have generated a different set of circumstances.

   Looking back, I wonder if my assistant was looking to the research base and drawing on professional literature in her approach to gain a sense of power from relying on authority. And as we failed to address the power imbalance and the students understood that I was their "main" teacher and started to bond with me accordingly, she likely felt left out and even more powerless to do what she was there to do, which was to support student learning.

   A good co-teaching relationship when a power imbalance is present will name that power imbalance outright and then together, both parties can discuss student-centered ways for everyone to contribute. So much of "best practice" in co-teaching suggests a 50/50 split of energy and duties is the solution, but perhaps a 100/100 split, where every educator in the room is regarded as having unique value to bring to bear, is more powerful.

3. Asking for help.

By the time I had a classroom of my own, I had a long list of achievements and the added pressure of a role as a lead teacher. Someone so accomplished and not only in charge of a room full of students but also in a leadership role with a co-teacher, in my mind, couldn't ask for help.

Yet if I had turned to a more experienced teacher or a mentor, I would likely have been afforded some of the same advice I could give today around conflict resolution and negotiating teaching responsibility that led to so much inner turmoil for me that year.

FURTHER RESOURCES

New York Times bestseller *Crucial Conversations: Tools for Talking When Stakes Are High* by Kerry Patterson, Joseph Grenny, Ron McMillan, and Al Switzler is a text that while not teaching specific, lays out clear steps to support constructive, supportive dialogue even when emotions are high and resolution feels far off.

Team Being: The Art and Science of Working Well With Others by Gary Gemmill and Michael Schoonmaker draws on scientific and practical insights the authors drew from years of working with creative teams in education, government, and business.

Moving from Teacher Isolation to Collaboration: Enhancing Professionalism and School Quality by Sharon Conley and Bruce Cooper is a text that illuminates the historical underpinnings of the phenomenon of teacher isolation including district and school structure and teacher accountability systems and explores the independent complexity of the teacher's role and how to move toward collaboration even in contexts that make such collaboration more difficult.

The Cult of Pedagogy has many helpful steps toward co-teaching harmony here: https://www.cultofpedagogy.com/co-teaching-push-in/

Chapter 13

There Is No Ethos

How I Learned to Stop Entitlement and Gain Student Trust

Mark DiMauro

English Faculty

Westmoreland County Community College

and University of Pittsburgh-Johnstown

I first stepped into the world of teaching and education in a manner, I would imagine, wholly different from most of my colleagues. Before completing my undergraduate degree, I left school for a time and went to work for a global retail company at a branch just outside Washington D.C.

While I was there, I was rapidly introduced to the world of electronics management—and all its myriad downsides—and this also marked my trek into the teaching profession. Though it seems a bit of a non sequitur, the retail environment (and management in a more general sense) is the practical equivalent of teaching, a world in which interpersonal skills, the ability to be simultaneously informative and entertaining, and the authority on a particular subject are not only invaluable but mandatory.

My success as a manager in this environment was no small component in my success as an educator, and the skills I learned, practiced, and perfected there remain essential to my own professional persona.

My previous boss at the same company had given me an indelible piece of advice when I received news I was being promoted: "Don't worry, the shirt carries a lot of authority." What he meant, of course, was that associates and customers alike responded to the grey manager's shirt differently than the standard black or red of a simple sales associate.

It was his own way of describing the way he felt his authority and how he applied it to his own management style. He believed the shirt granted him authority and credibility to his interactions. I took his words to heart, and therein lay my biggest miscalculation.

I had an assumption that because I had been promoted it was a way that corporate was recognizing me both for good service and as an acknowledgement that I was good at my job, and thus the associates to whom I was to give direction would also recognize that fact. My new position required me to travel to different stores, in addition to having my own "home store," in an attempt to train associates and boost flagging sales at other branches.

I was under the mistaken impression—bolstered, of course, by the advice I had received—that the shirt was somehow "magical." That by simply placing the thin, poorly manufactured grey threads upon my torso, I was conferred incredible "manager powers" that accompanied a set of store keys and an alarm code.

Slicing away the drama, I believed, for lack of a better term, that being a manager *meant* something to anyone other than myself. There was no ethos— no inherent credibility or trustworthiness—to being a manager, and much the same applies to being a teacher.

My expectation of authority wasn't to last.

The first few months were very rough, to put it mildly. Associates bucked beneath me when I didn't provide them transparent rationale for the tasks I would delegate. My sales methods, which I knew worked and were reliable, were rejected simply because they were foreign. Customers saw the shirt not as a symbol of authority but as a doormat, upon which they could eagerly launch an assortment of complaints, accusations, and rude comments.

A host of reports and metrics showed, plainly, that I was good at my job. The company knew I was an asset; they had rewarded me with this promotion. My mistake was believing that I was somehow entitled to customer or associate respect simply by virtue of my position.

There are any number of platitudes one can make here: that respect is earned and not given, not to ask an employee to do anything that you weren't willing to do yourself, and so on. The key for me, however, and what has lasted onward into my new career, were three lessons I acquired once I recognized my errors. Fortunately, I had a massive network arrayed in front of me—with my livelihood on the line as punishment for straying too far—that was more than willing to point out my mistakes.

It had become clear that I needed to change the way I managed. I had to stop believing that being a manager (read: teacher) meant anything. Being the one in charge simply means being the one at whom the fingers are pointed when it all goes wrong—it was my job to make sure that didn't happen, and the only way I could accomplish that goal was with a team, a team which first needed to buy in to what we were all there trying to accomplish.

If this sounds familiar to the classroom setting (where my second career brought me after a decade), then you've earned a gold star; getting your students to believe in and trust you is the first, last, and (almost) only job of the teacher. Communicating content is a primary aspect of an effective teacher in a quality classroom, but one cannot effectively communicate content until one is able to gain this trust of the audience.

The most important lesson I learned was the value of purpose. I needed to be tactful when speaking to associates, and I needed to be tactful when speaking to students. Tact, as it is famously described, is the ability to make a point without making an enemy. Getting agreement from someone isn't necessarily all about wholly altering a point of view or creating a sea change in perspective. Sometimes acquiring buy-in from a student is as simple as asking them to give it a try.

This lesson materialized after a multitude of failed attempts that boiled down to simple tautologies – versions of "because I said so," or, in this case, "because I'm the manager"—and it wasn't until I became more transparent with my purposes behind tasks and assignments that students began to buy in. Teachers can enact this point by explicitly explaining the reason why students are given the assignments we give them. Nothing is more antithetical to student buy-in than "busy work," perceived or real.

Note that this buy-in is far more easily acquired when students understand not just *what* it is they're doing but *why*. No one enjoys having their time wasted, and an assignment with opaque or confusing motives can feel like exactly that. If I wasn't clear and direct about my directives and their purpose, my associates (read: students) would ignore me. If I wasn't explicit about reasoning, frustration was born.

Students need to "learn how to learn" almost as much as they need the content you are providing, and one of the best and most direct ways to accomplish is to not only tell your students what to do but to emphasize the logic behind it. If you didn't spell it out, you can't be frustrated that they didn't pick up on it. They can't read your mind, so tell them.

Ask yourself of every assignment you put into your syllabus: "What's the reasoning behind this assignment?" If you can't answer the question immediately, or have some sort of vague, jargon-filled nonanswer, then you need to review your lesson and try again.

If there was a meaningfulness scale for assignments, busy work would be at the bottom next to review, and somewhere near the top would be "valuable and generative content examinations."

That is, activities that promote critical thinking, strong analytical and evaluative skills, useful cross-references to other literature and other fields of study, and, perhaps most importantly, an ability to situate what you're learning to the pragmatic world—an explanation, as it were, of "why this matters" or "how you might use this moving forward in your education and/ or employment."

A simple question from a student illuminates this point. As I was creating my syllabus for a Composition I class, my first ever teaching assignment, I asked several other teachers to look it over and provide feedback.

Are there too many lessons? Am I giving myself too much to grade? Is there enough group work/too much group work?

This was the type of formative criticism I was after. Most teachers gave some basic feedback, some minor edits, and some recommendations. Feeling confident, I brought the syllabus into class and distributed it.

Before class was over, however, my entire perspective had shifted. I was explaining the assignments on the syllabus—one, in particular, was a discussion on the proper format and layout of thesis statements—a lesson which I had included in my section on narrative essays.

One student raised a hand. "Why do we need a thesis statement for a narrative essay?" she asked. I stopped momentarily. *Because every essay needs a thesis*, my brain said. *Because you need to learn how to properly write one . . . because I couldn't fit it anywhere else in our schedule . . .* I wracked my brain, feeling awkward because I didn't have an immediate answer.

Finally, I sighed. "You don't," I replied. "But it's something we'll be working with later on." I knew, immediately, that my sequencing was off. Students expected the thesis lesson to relate directly to their first essay (their narrative essay), and when it didn't things began to feel disjointed.

I edited my syllabus that evening and distributed new copies the next class session, this time with the thesis lesson moved to better reflect the persuasive genre essay in which it should have reasonably first appeared. That single question, "Why?" as in "Why are we doing this?" made me pause and realize that I didn't have an answer—and that wasn't good enough for them, which meant it wasn't good enough for me.

I got something of a valuable experience in teaching before ever stepping foot into a classroom. Chances are good that you did too, if you think back to your own life experience and draw from it. Even if it isn't formalized education, it likely brought with it a subset of interpersonal (and other) skills that remain viable and valuable.

After all, convincing your students to listen to you is your number one goal as a teacher—otherwise, nothing else you say will matter to them even a single iota. Whether you decide to accomplish this through humor, engagement, challenge, or gamesmanship is up to you.

Just remember that your students won't listen to you "just because" you're their teacher. That grey shirt is *not* magic and has no ethos. It means absolutely nothing.

FURTHER RESOURCES

If you're interested in reading more about getting student buy-in to your lessons, I would recommend you look outside of pedagogical resources and at resources that provide valuable performative information: acting, public speech, body language, comedy.

Pedagogy is, of course, the essential part of our jobs, but without obtaining student buy-in it is all but wasted. Learning and practicing these speech and entertainment skills ensures that your students are invested in whatever it is you're discussing, and there is perhaps no better way to learn it than from those whose primary job is as an entertainer.

Try filming yourself during your lessons and watch it back to see where you may have gone wrong; practice asking and answering questions, and be ready to say "I don't know"—it is perfectly acceptable for a teacher to admit a limit to his or her knowledge base. You'll drive student buy-in far more through honesty than through expertise.

Part IV

CREATING RESPONSIVE ENVIRONMENTS FOR STUDENT LEARNING

Chapter 14

Trigger Warnings

Alaina Smith, MA

Program Coordinator, William H Thompson
Scholars Learning Community
University of Nebraska, Lincoln

If you know a teacher, you've most likely heard someone say, "I'm in it for the kids," or "It's not about the paycheck," or "I just want to leave a lasting impact on the world." These were all reasons why I signed up to be a classroom teacher. No one believed Mandela's words more than me: Education is the most powerful weapon which you can use to change the world. I was in the classroom to change the world, as were many of my fellow teachers.

The change I was most interested in was justice.

College had awakened me to language that helped me understand the oppression I had always felt as a Black woman, and I brought ideas of liberation into the classroom, eager to dismantle harmful systems through the texts assigned to students.

"Shouldn't you be nervous about tackling these topics with 13- and 14-year-olds?" some would ask.

"Afraid? I'm here to empower!" would more or less be my reply. "Why be afraid of that?"

It wasn't that I didn't realize it would be uncomfortable. I knew talking with students about identity, power, and community would be challenging and difficult, but I also knew it would be good for my students as it had been for me.

I cannot remember a teacher of my own who had taught me I had intrinsic value *and also* that I was living in a world not set up for me. I felt gaslit my whole life being told, "Alaina, you are important and a valuable member of society as is everyone else," only to experience a world that often made me feel small because "you know how black people are" or "women just aren't cut out for this."

Using texts to disrupt students' acceptance of the status quo was a personal mission and every bit as important as teaching them literary devices, plot structure, and the use of citations. My students would walk out knowing they had value *and* they had a right to demand the world *see* that value.

And I made it to my fourth year of teaching without incident; it was then that I was shaken up a bit in my boots of justice. I was teaching the novel *Speak* by Laurie Halse Anderson to freshmen students.

In *Speak*, Anderson writes about a freshman in high school, Melinda, who was raped by an upperclassman at a summer party before classes began. She arrives at high school mute, unable to share what has happened to her with anyone. *Speak* is a novel about how Melinda finds her voice and power over the course of her first year of high school.

It was my second school year teaching *Speak* and the year before it had been the text that generated the most student interest. This year I was so proud of how a coworker and I had streamlined the unit into a workbook. My students were about to understand bodily autonomy and how to write a thematic essay. Your girl was ready.

The unit began with an anticipation guide that was meant to pique students' interest in the book, set the stage for the themes of the novel, and uncover some of their own biases and misconceptions regarding sexual assault. Yes. I know. That's a lot to tackle in one class.

Nevertheless, we began with the students evaluating statements such as "If a victim of sexual assault does not fight back, they must have thought the assault was not that bad or they wanted it" and "If someone says 'no' they mean 'maybe' or are just playing hard to get." Students would label each statement as fact or myth. Then we discussed each statement as a class with students walking to one side of the room if they thought it was a myth and the other if they thought it was a fact.

Students were instructed to remain serious or they would be asked to leave, and they complied. There were of course some exclamations of surprise and nervous giggles, but students were engaged and mostly respectful. It was clear there were a lot of misconceptions around consent and sexual assault, and we discussed and built some clarity before we began reading the text, allowing students to approach Melinda's situation with an understanding of key definitions and expectations. It was a lot, but it was going so well.

Until the last class of the day.

Things were going as they had in my other classes, and then suddenly my student walked out of the room in tears.

The minute they walked out, I worried that I had triggered some horrible memory for this student. I asked a couple of their friends to check on them while I got the class to complete the activity.

Finally, able to check in with the student, my worries were confirmed. Discussing sexual assault brought back past trauma.

It had never been my intention. I wanted to help *prevent* trauma and not retraumatize. But in that moment intentions didn't matter, only impacts were salient.

Before leaving for the day, I talked to my student and made sure that they were okay. I apologized and was forgiven. Still, I felt terrible. I called that student's parent and had a conversation with them, apologizing again. Forgiven again, I still felt terrible.

I went to talk to our school counselor and we discussed what happened and came up with a game plan together in how to proceed with the unit. I wanted to avoid hurting students when what I had designed was a unit to empower.

As for the student who had survived trauma, we provided them with the opportunity to complete the unit on their own with a different text of their choice. They would sit in class for any lessons on writing, grammar, vocabulary, and so on and then work in the library when we discussed the text. This was an option the student was completely on board with.

We also presented this opportunity to other students, and I made it clear to them that no student should feel like they had to sit through something that would be traumatic for them. We sent home passive consent letters to parents making them aware of what was happening if they wanted to opt their student out.

The unit was taught and we all got through it. In fact, once again, *Speak* was the most popular text of the school year.

Yet this experience represented an awakening. While the battle I was fighting to empower students remained central, I was suddenly nervous that I had been doing as much harm as good in my efforts. In this age of MeToo and BlackLivesMatter it was crucial I was doing the work that moved the collective forward. This incident, though, forced me to set aside my intentions and focus on my impact.

I had spent several years absorbing information on the treatment of marginalized people, and it had provided me with clarity and direction, but I had not spent time thinking about how to introduce that information to over one hundred distinct individuals who each bring their own knowledge and lived experiences with them.

Teachers cannot center each individual student in their teaching. Classrooms can and will never be a one-on-one conversation with any one student. But we can try to make sure each student is allowed to take up the space in a conversation that they want to take. If we want to empower students, we can give them power over their level of involvement in those conversations.

This doesn't mean that students who opt to read a different text and write their essay in the library are not engaged or learning, and it doesn't mean they don't value the issue that they cannot be present for.

My student who fled the classroom was insistent that *Speak* should continue to be taught because clearly there were people in the class and school who did not understand consent and sexual assault. They probably valued that text and the accompanying conversations as much if not more than any other member of that class, but for their own well-being could not participate.

My reflection also made me realize that as an adult, I opt out of important conversations sometimes too. As a Black person there are some texts that depict the trauma Black people face that I just cannot handle because they are emotionally overwhelming for me.

There are other ways for me to engage in the conversation on race. Sometimes I can read a text, but I cannot discuss it in the presence of others, particularly white people. It is too much for me. I value those texts. I want them to be read and discussed. I just can't do it myself.

Teachers should provide a preview for each text, warning students of whatever was coming in a book that could be possibly harmful for them. To build confidence in students who wanted to be in the room but were wary, teachers can spend time building context.

When teaching *A Mighty Long Way*, Carlotta Walls Lanier's memoir about her experience as a member of the Little Rock Nine, for example, teachers can take a lot of time providing not only the context for what was happening at that moment in history, but also building protocols for how to discuss race in the classroom. Ensure that Black students know that their emotional responses are valid, and if they need space, they can have it.

Asking for help is something teachers can do when surmounting difficult topics in the classroom. School counselors can help teachers develop materials, and school resource officers can discuss legal definitions of topics such as sexual assault. The perspective of licensed counselors and other professionals in realigning course units can be extremely helpful. With more support, teachers can build even stronger units with more intentional support for students.

In the case of *A Mighty Long Way*, for instance, a required text for all eighth-grade classrooms across many districts, teachers uncomfortable teaching civil rights history but wanting to make sure all of their students felt safe in their classrooms might reach out to their district's Office of Equity Affairs or similar body for support in designing a unit. Many beginning teachers are insistent they must do it all on their own. But teachers need a community to support students and students benefit when they see teachers lean on their community.

Also important is what teachers choose to teach. Texts that center on themes of gender, race, sexuality, class, or similar, often traffic in the trauma experienced by marginalized groups. Teachers should be intentional about selecting texts that show the world their joy, ingenuity, creativity, and community. Texts that unpack masculinity, white supremacy, and homophobia in ways that put the focus on the roots of those issues and not on the pain that they cause are wonderful choices for classrooms.

Along those lines, an excellent companion text to *Speak* would be Elizabeth Acevedo's *With Fire on High*, a book that is joyful and fun and also provides a path to talk about sex and consent in the classroom but in the context of a healthy relationship between two characters and not one of abuse. There are authors creating books with pathways to difficult issues that are triumphant, funny, communal, and equally as powerful.

Educators can tend to be fearful of teaching controversial and difficult topics in secondary education. There are fears that treating these texts can harm students, and indeed they can. But my experience also taught me that my mistake wasn't in what I aimed to do but how I did it. It taught me that it's okay to make a mistake. It's important to take a step back, reassess, apologize, and ask for help when mistakes happen. And it's important to keep trying.

It can be unnerving and even deterring having a lesson so well-meaning go so wrong, but that shouldn't stop educators from having the conversations with students that inspired their choice in becoming a teacher in the first place. The more I engage with students the more I agree with Mandela. Education is the most powerful tool, which is why I have to be careful with how I use it.

FURTHER RESOURCES

Private Readings in Public: Schooling the Literary Imagination by Dennis Sumara is a classic text that explores the complexities inherent to schooled readings of literature amidst the diversity of lived experiences within the classroom.

The concept of trigger warnings itself has been explored in professional literature from a variety of perspectives: as a social justice issue, as an issue of academic freedom, and within the scope of a pedagogy of care that attends to students' physical and emotional boundaries.

Teachers interested in the topic can access a landscape of texts that discuss how to handle difficult and potentially retraumatizing topics in the classroom with sensitivity and in a way that they feel prepared to support students.[1]

Race Talk in the Age of the Trigger Warning: Recognizing and Challenging Classroom Cultures of Silence by Mara Lee Grayson is a text that challenges the utility and equity of trigger warnings and raises questions about how classroom practice can support transformative dialogue. Work by Leland Spencer and Theresa Kulbaga highlights the ways in which trigger warnings serve to expand the circle of who can access academic content by supporting safe spaces for learning where students have confidence educators will take care not to retraumatize them in the classroom environment.[2] Glenn Singleton's work on "Courageous Conversation" is invaluable in building competency around discussing race specifically in classrooms.

NOTES

1. Wolfsdorf, A., Scott, A., & Herzog, S. (2019). What happened on July 21st: An investigation of trauma and trigger warnings in the English classroom. *Changing English*, 26(2), 198–215.

2. Spencer, L. G., & Kulbaga, T. A. (2018). Trigger warnings as respect for student boundaries in university classrooms. *Journal of Curriculum and Pedagogy*, *15*(1), 106–122.

Chapter 15

Dealing with Math Anxiety

Bobson Wong
Math Teacher, New York City Public Schools
Master Teacher, Math for America

One of the biggest mistakes I've made is to underestimate *math anxiety*, the feelings of fear and apprehension that people experience when doing math. As a math teacher, I've seen it in many forms over the years—people who admit to me that they were "bad at math" in school, parents who feel uncomfortable helping their children with their math homework, or students who are too discouraged to pay attention in math class.

At first, I believed that my students could overcome their math anxiety if I simply provided clear mathematical instruction. However, trying to get students to see those mathematical connections wasn't enough for many struggling learners. I couldn't figure out what to do—until my challenges dealing with one of my students led me to question my beliefs about math and teaching.

When I started teaching, I believed that being good at math wasn't related to how you felt about it. "Math is objective," another teacher reassured me. "Emotions don't affect how you do math. You just need to know how to do it."

I thought that students who struggled in math just didn't see its logic. Thus, my lessons contained not just procedures but also explanations of why those procedures made sense. I talked enthusiastically about math, hoping that my energy could be transferred to students.

Emphasizing the connections between topics would enable them to appreciate the beauty of math and improve their academic performance. My students praised my meticulous planning, energy for talking about math, and ability to state mathematical concepts clearly. I focused on answering their questions and re-explaining concepts when they didn't understand. I thought that just doing this would be good enough to be an effective teacher, so I didn't worry about how they *felt* about math.

I also believed that maintaining discipline would also help students learn by keeping them focused. To me, teachers who befriended students blurred the boundaries between adults and children. Small talk during the lesson wasted valuable class time that could be better spent discussing mathematics. As a result, I was very strict in the classroom. Over time, I became more relaxed, but I maintained an emotional distance from them. I believed that getting to know students better could undermine my authority.

No matter how hard I tried, though, some students always remained out of reach. These students had done poorly in previous math courses, usually failing at least once. With weak computational skills, they had managed to pass by learning mnemonics and test-taking techniques.

Although they kept up with my classwork at the beginning of the year, they usually stopped working as the material got harder. I tried explaining the material in different ways, encouraging them to get tutoring, and reaching out to their parents and guidance counselors, but nothing seemed to work.

My difficulties with a student named John made me rethink the way in which I taught math. He was in my class of students who had failed the course. Since this was a class of repeaters, I put a great deal of effort into planning lessons for John's class, thinking about ways to connect what we discussed to other mathematical ideas.

However, class didn't seem to engage him. He didn't have a notebook and would only occasionally write down a few calculations or words onto the classwork sheets that I gave out every day. At the end of the period, his classwork could usually be found on the floor or in the garbage can—an indication that he didn't think it was worth keeping.

John had trouble keeping up with the work. When students worked independently, he often called me over to explain the problems that I had just explained to the class during my lesson. This frustrated me since I felt that he should have paid attention to me the first time that I said it and resented what I felt was the drain on my attention that I could have spent helping other students.

Meanwhile, I could see that he couldn't follow my lessons because he didn't understand many mathematical ideas that he should have learned last year and the year before.

One day, speaking to John privately, I pointed out that he needed extra help. "In order for me to explain everything to you properly, I need more time than I can give you in class," I said. "Perhaps you could go to tutoring during your lunch period."

John shook his head. "I've always been bad at math," he answered. "I went to tutoring before and it didn't help."

His response sounded to me like a selfish cry for individual attention. "Well, I can't really spend the entire period explaining every problem just to you," I snapped. "What about the 30 other students in the class?"

John lowered his head and shrugged his shoulders. He left the room with a defeated look on his face.

After that conversation, John's behavior and classwork deteriorated. He started loud arguments with other students across the room. He frequently came late to class, immediately asked to go to the bathroom, and then disappeared for 30 minutes. John often took out his phone to text his friends or play video games. He stopped coming to class regularly and failed the course.

One day near the end of the school year, I complained to a colleague about John's behavior. She replied that she had students that behaved the same way and suggested that he may have math anxiety.

For a long time, I resisted the idea of connecting my students' academic difficulties to their fear of math. I had heard about math anxiety, but I dismissed it as an emotion that students could overcome with clear instruction and better focus.

As I learned more about math anxiety, I realized that it was more than a feeling. People with math anxiety display a variety of physiological symptoms, including sweaty palms, increased heart rate, nausea, and headaches. These symptoms inhibit cognitive functions and reduce memory capacity, which affect the ability to retain new information.

In her book *Overcoming Math Anxiety*, Sheila Tobias points out that people with math anxiety often fear that asking questions would reveal their lack of understanding. Their desire to avoid being exposed leaves them feeling ashamed and intimidated.

Failing to acknowledge the fears of students like John created a barrier to learning that they couldn't easily overcome, no matter how interesting or clear classroom lessons were. Clearly, a different approach was needed.

Research indicates that in order to address students' math anxiety, teachers must develop meaningful relationships with them. Positive student–teacher relationships can improve students' self-esteem and lower the feelings of tension that create physiological obstacles to learning. In contrast, maintaining an emotional distance from students can lower their motivation and persistence.

As I learned more about math anxiety, I realized that I had misjudged John. Instead of questioning why he was so disengaged in class, I had relied solely on the quality of my instruction to motivate him and had dismissed his constantly calling me over for help as "attention-seeking" behavior, when he was probably looking for a way to connect with me.

I suspect that he was trying to show me that he wanted to do well, but he may have been afraid to admit that he lacked many basic mathematical skills. I should have spent more time talking to him, even about things that had nothing to do with math. Furthermore, if I had provided better academic support—using my conversations with him to identify his level of understanding and then adjusting my lessons to build up his mathematical skills—he could have felt less anxious and could have been more motivated to work.

Teachers can implement small steps to treat students as individuals rather than impersonal vessels into which they pour mathematical knowledge. For instance, as they fill out the information sheet that teachers often administer to students to fill out on the first day of class, teachers can ask them to describe what aspects of math made them hopeful and what made them afraid.

Greeting each student by name every day and regularly engaging in small talk with them can also support students with math anxiety. When students don't know something that they are supposed to have learned before or when they take out their cell phones in class, avoid taking it as a personal insult or conclude that students were being "disrespectful." Instead, spend more time thinking about and identifying *why* they act in particular ways.

I employed these approaches and discovered many things about my students that wouldn't have been possible otherwise.

One student wanted to be a psychologist because she liked talking to people and wanted to understand what they were thinking.

Another was always tired in class because he had to work after school at his father's restaurant.

One girl had an excellent intuition for estimation that nobody had identified because she didn't know how to explain her reasoning, so she was often dismissed as "uncooperative."

A student stopped doing work and started acting out in class because his mother had been recently diagnosed with cancer.

Many students had developed reputations as "difficult" because nobody believed that they were willing to learn.

Connecting with students improves the classroom environment and student academic performance. Students disrupt lessons less frequently and listen more when they sense that the teacher cares about them. Knowing more about their likes and dislikes can also help teachers customize lessons to match student interests, which in turn improves their motivation. Teachers should acknowledge student math anxiety by reassuring them that struggle is a normal part of mathematical work and showing them techniques that previous students found helpful.

Of course, these strategies aren't foolproof. There will always be days when students have difficulty with a lesson. Despite a teacher's best efforts, some students will still fail.

Overall, though, students and teachers will be more motivated once teachers recognize the importance of addressing students' fear of math. Furthermore, many students a teacher might previously have written off as hopeless may end up not just passing the course but actually *excelling*. Developing meaningful personal relationships with students is an important first step to reducing their math anxiety.

FURTHER RESOURCES

Overcoming Math Anxiety by Sheila Tobias, though written over four decades ago, endures as one of the most powerful analyses of what makes math difficult for some. After all, it's the book that brought the term "math anxiety" into popular usage.

Mathematical Mindsets: Unleashing Students' Potential through Creative Math, Inspiring Messages and Innovative Teaching by Jo Boaler describes approaches to curriculum and instruction that provide support for math anxious students.

.

Chapter 16

Interrupting Binary Thinking in a Trauma-Informed Elementary Classroom

Kate Haq, PhD
English Language Arts & Social Studies Educator
The Park School of Buffalo, New York

Dale was an eight-year-old student in my classroom who came from a home in which he was the only male in a sea of sisters. His mom was a graduate student and the family lived together with her boyfriend on the Native reservation down the street from the elementary school.

Dale was brilliant and needed constant challenging academic work to stimulate and sustain him during the school day. But he was an unhappy boy who often lashed out at other students and adults, acting dismissive of most of the girls and pestering the boys to be his friend. He, like many students, had experienced trauma in his short lifetime, and his behavior allowed a window into this thinking and personal history.

His reputation preceded him, as I had heard about Dale's disruptive classroom behavior from other teachers in the lunchroom. However, I liked to rely on my relationship-building skills rather than hearsay and never read a child's permanent record until well after the first semester.

In addition, I had two young boys of my own at home and as a white woman, I had invested time and effort in learning about and incorporating Haudenosaunee culture and traditions into my classroom. I felt confident this student and I would eventually create a learning environment within which we could both thrive. This goal would take time and flexible, personal interactions with Dale over many days. Unfortunately, before we had much of a chance to develop our relationship, something occurred that set us back.

Our building had a new vice principal that year and his role was that of disciplinarian. He was shared between grades three and five in our building and six through eight in the adjoining middle school. I rarely, if ever, sent anyone to the office for discipline, as I preferred to create conditions that led to a supportive environment for all. September was well under way and I had not yet met him on a personal level, when "Mr. B" appeared at my door and interrupted my grammar mini-lesson asking for Dale.

I busied the students with a turn and talk while I met Mr. B at the door, explaining that if he could let me know the nature of the problem he had with Dale, I might be able to address it within the confines of my classroom. I did not want Dale to be removed from the classroom, as many of his cohort had already labeled him "trouble" based on this type of previous interaction with adults.

I was working toward helping Dale craft a new image for himself as a stellar student who knew so much the teacher depended on his input in subjects ranging from mathematics to Native history.

Unfortunately, Mr. B did not know this or me or Dale. His mission included the binary of good/bad kids and he would not be dissuaded. Binary thinking is part of human nature, as we mentally categorize in binary terms for quick understanding of people, situations, and choices.

And although the National Education Association (NEA) promotes administrators as educational academic leaders, the reality in schools is that student and faculty discipline consume much of building level administrators' time and energy. Mr. B was specifically hired as a disciplinarian and his job called for quick judgement and swift solutions, hence binary thinking.

Mr. B loudly commanded Dale to get out of his seat and come to the classroom door and Dale refused. This interaction immediately escalated the tension in the room, as I continued to advocate for the ability to address the perceived rule breaking later on within my classroom. The class of 26 students began to buzz. I could see all of my hard work over the past three weeks exploding out of the classroom as Mr. B physically grabbed Dale by the arm and hauled him out the door, while Dale toppled his desk.

I was near tears as I heard Dale grabbing onto lockers screaming "I didn't do anything!" as the grown administrator dragged him down the hallway.

I immediately called my principal, with whom I had a decent relationship, and asked for an aide to release me from my classroom so that I could be present in the office while Dale was being interviewed. Nobody was available, so after talking to the class about withholding judgement, we returned to our grammar lesson with heavy hearts.

You see, Mr. B could only envision me as an elementary classroom teacher—not a highly skilled decision-maker, veteran educator, or colleague—just a woman unequipped to deal with a perceived "bad boy." And it seemed he could only see himself as a disciplinarian—not a collaborator, listener, or culturally sensitive educator—trying to start his administrative career as a decisive white man.

Needless to say, there was a great deal to discuss with Mr. B after school that day. I brought Dale's thick, unread file with me to the meeting and shared stories of my own interactions with his family members, the Native liaison, and our progress so far together as teachers and learners of each other. It was a frustrating meeting because tempers were high and both Mr. B and I felt misunderstood by each other.

I told Mr. B that he was not welcome in my classroom and that if he needed to speak with one of my students, he must allow me to be present. He was astonished at my assertions, which he perceived as bold and unusual, and he threatened to write me up for insubordination. Finally, our principal appeared from across the hall to put an end to the contentious meeting and ushered me out.

I was furious and spent the evening telling my husband about the unseasoned, brutish young new administrator who I was never going to forgive for mistreating my student and dismissing me as insubordinate. I knew I had failed to convey my work with Dale in a way that brought Mr. B around to my way of thinking and educating and that my temper was both a tool and a vice.

As a teacher, I was able to see the complexity of my students, their needs, and individual selves but often did not extend this comprehensive way of thinking to adults. I admit to a binary way of thinking that includes kids = good, adults = bad. We are all judgmental and often we make decisions about people from initial encounters that color our ways of viewing them for an extended period of time.

So it was in my relationship with Mr. B. We avoided each other for most of that school year until one May morning when I returned from dropping the class off in the gym to find Mr. B sitting on my desk in the darkened empty classroom.

He sincerely apologized for his behavior those many months ago and commended me for my work with Dale and described me as a master teacher. He admitted to not knowing the culture of the school or community and confessed that his heavy handiness stemmed from fear of failure.

I was stunned at his openness, his desire to explain himself, and his willingness to embrace his culpability and poor behavior. I, in turn, reiterated my intense desire to reach every child and acknowledged that my temper may have influenced my ability to work to resolve our issues.

When he asked my thoughts on how he might begin to build a relationship with Dale, I realized how much Mr. B had grown in a relatively short amount of time. My binary view of Mr. B as administrator = obstacle expanded to include learner, listener, and—over time—trusted colleague.

There is much complexity inherent to relationship building among students, families, teachers, and administrators in a public elementary school. Binary thinking often constricts our view of possibilities and advances notions that shut down dialogue.

The next time you are in a faculty meeting or professional development, spend some time sharing binary views you have with each other. They may be as simple as "public schools should teach cursive writing" or "non-gendered gym classes are not appropriate."

Once these unconscious biases are dragged into the light of day, we can begin to see how they bind our thinking into either/or instead of what if? and yes, and.

Shannon Hale, author of the Princess Academy books, spoke passionately about the binary nature of boy books versus girl books in Grace Lin's #KidLitWomen podcast and illustrates one aspect of the binary culture of schooling. Shannon moved from the personal nature of hate-filled disgust that some elementary school boys exhibited as they spoke of her "girly" books, to the structural deficiencies within schools that characterize good (male) versus bad (female).

Shannon extended her thinking into race in public schooling, where white students are not necessarily asked to read from other perspectives while kids of color have been required to do so since the birth of American public schooling (i.e., after kids of color were allowed into public schools).

These are just a couple of examples of the binary nature of educational thinking, but it comes in many forms. One of the most harmful binaries is the hierarchy of schooling itself, which privileges administrator decision-making over teachers' and students'.

Paulo Freire described dialogue and dialogic educational settings as spaces where, together through dialogue, we co-create new knowledge; where

Table 16.1   Further Resources

Resources for Adults	Resources for Students
A Deep Conversation about Binary Thinking by Allie Jane Bruce	Cheng, J. (2017). *See You in the Cosmos*. New York, NY: Dial Publishing. (middle grades)
Educators' Guide for Stamped by Reynolds & Kendi	Craft, J. (2019). *New Kid*. New York, NY: HarperCollins. (middle grades)
Countering Binary Thinking by Dr. Suzanne Simon	Dunbar-Ortiz, R. (2019). *An Indigenous Peoples' History of the United States for Young People*. Boston, MA: Beacon Press. (YA, ages 12+)
Psychology Today, When Binary Thinking Is Involved, Polarization Follows	Ireland, J. (2019). *Dread Nation*. London: Titan Books. (YA, ages 12+)
What Are We Really Saying to Our Children? by Maya Gonzalez	Reynolds, J., & Kendi, I. (2020). *Stamped: Racism, Anti-racism, and You*. New York, NY: Hatchette Book Group and other titles by Jason Reynolds. (YA, ages 12+)
Grace Lin's KidLitPodcast	
Au, W. (2012). *Critical Curriculum Studies: Education, Consciousness, and the Politics of Knowing*. New York, NY: Routledge.	Rivera, G. (2019). *Juliet Takes a Breath*. London: Penguin. (YA, ages 12+)
	Smith, A. A. (2014). *Grasshopper Jungle: A History*. New York, NY: Dutton Books. (YA, ages 12+)
Iantaffi, A., & Barker, M. J. (2019). *Life Isn't Binary: On Being Both, Beyond, and In-between*. London: Jessica Kingsley Publishers.	Williams-Garcia, R., & Johnson, S. A. (2010). *One Crazy Summer*. New York, NY: Amistad and other titles by Rita Williams-Garcia. (middle grades)
Shor, I., & P. Freire. (1987). What is the 'dialogical method' of teaching? *Journal of Education 169*, 3, 11–31.	Woodson, J. (2018). *Harbor Me*. London: Penguin and other titles by Jacqueline Woodson. (primary, middle, and YA books)
	Zinn, H. (2011). *A Young People's History of the United States: Columbus to the War on Terror*. New York, NY: Seven Stories Press. (middle grades, YA)

"dialogue is a moment where humans meet to reflect on their reality as they make and remake it."

Public schools are, of course, the ideal setting for this knowledge creation to occur, but if we are to honor all participants, teachers must become learners while learners become teachers. Too often, adults adopt binary thinking about their role, whether it be teacher or administrator, and this exclusionary thinking prevents them from expanding their understanding of themselves in ways that open up dialogue with students, families, and each other.

FURTHER RESOURCES

Expanding perspectives and moving away from ingrained binary thinking involves deliberate curricular choices and resources. Books and resources that introduce marginalized perspectives can be helpful for children and adults since we so often encounter the white, typically male, point of view.

Asking ourselves and our students to think about who is left out of a story or historical retelling can generate alternative perspectives and expand thinking in critical ways, as multicultural and multi-gendered perspectives can disrupt binary thinking for all of us.

As a literacy specialist, I designed the chart below to supply educators with readings for themselves and their colleagues around critical thinking beyond the binary, as well as resources for students.

Chapter 17

Learning to Overcome Dysfunctional Independence

Peter Warner
Retired Professor of Computer Science

A few years out of college, I started my own custom software development business—something I was good at and enjoyed very much. Since it would take a while before I could find enough work to keep me fully occupied, I kept my eyes open for any suitable for part-time work.

Within a couple of weeks, a job teaching computer programming at a local technical school became available. Perfect! The fact I had absolutely no formal educational training gave me little pause. After all, I had just spent some sixteen years observing teachers. Besides, I knew the subject cold and had taught several seminar classes at my four-year university. What could go wrong?

To be clear, I did realize that teaching a semester-long class compared to a one-day seminar was a different kettle of fish. But I had confidence that my basic approach to teaching technical subjects would still work: create interest, establish a framework, and then build on that framework brick by brick. I also knew teaching took planning and, to ensure everything started off smoothly, I spent two long weeks preparing for just the first three lessons.

On the first day of class, about 20 students showed up—all adults of varying ages. I delivered my welcoming remarks and provided an overview of the class and then dove into my first sure-to-be-fascinating lesson.

After a few minutes, though, I noticed eyes across the classroom starting to glaze over. Those students that didn't look completely dazed were leaning back in their chairs, arms crossed, with an expression "of teach me something" on their faces. The second day was more of the same, with a few students even dozing off.

At first, I entered a phase where I blamed the students. These aren't the kinds of motivated students I expected, I thought.

Next, I panicked. I was sure that my approach was solid, and I felt confident in what I was doing in the classroom. So what exactly was going wrong?

Then, one day, as if by magic, my ego receded. Or maybe it finally just became so clear that I needed help that I could no longer continue to operate as I had been.

As an entrepreneur I was used to solving problems, concocting solutions for my clients, and working alone. These qualities can be fruitful but in this case they were an impediment to my ability to get the help I clearly needed.

I went to the program director's office and laid bare that I was going down in flames and simply did not know how to recover. To my great relief, she didn't indicate that she regretted hiring me or seem alarmed at my incompetence. Instead, she smiled and then patiently asked me a few questions about what was going on in the classroom. From her demeanor and questions, I knew right away she was there to support me rather than criticize my approach or lecture to me about pedagogy.

What came next was rock solid advice, all of which was entirely actionable. I walked out of her office with a sense of relief—I could fix this and, furthermore, someone had my back if I needed more help.

So what did she tell me?

The first point she made was a fact that had eluded me despite just how key it was: for the most part, the students that found themselves enrolled in our technical school had a pattern of academic failure going back for years and it was our job to try to turn this pattern around. She also explained that while our typical students lacked academic confidence, there were simple methods for building feelings of efficacy that would help them access my content.

Her advice amounted to this:

- break my lectures and projects down to bite-size pieces,
- assign lots of doable homework and go over it in class each day, and
- employ frequent quizzes so students could see their progress.

The director explained that smaller projects, doable homework, and frequent quizzes would all serve to build confidence—in both my students and me.

I resolved to abandon the model of do-or-die, high stakes tests full of arcane questions that tested your IQ rather than your mastery of the course material. From that day forward, anyone who chose to fully participate would succeed, I promised myself.

In practice, this meant that my homework and daily quizzes matched my lectures and projects with strict alignment. Going over each homework assignment and quiz in class offered students opportunities to ask questions and to reinforce the material from the day before. The frequency of the quizzes gave my students feedback on any course corrections that needed to be made and I could see if I needed to make adjustments in how I was covering a topic.

By design, too, all questions on the exams were taken from the quizzes without exception. I let my students know this, implicitly communicating that if one paid attention, completed homework assignments, and did well on the quizzes, passing the class was attainable. This would motivate students to take the quizzes seriously and give them some confidence that they could pass no matter their prior experience with the course content, which would amount to more confidence building as I sought to turn a pattern of failure into a pattern of success.

The transformation of my class was almost instantaneous. All but a handful latched onto what was happening and we started to have lively, productive classes. It was work for all of us but the constant feeling of accomplishment made it enjoyable.

As I write this, I have sitting on my desk an engraved pewter mug given to me when my final class found out I was leaving after a year and a half of teaching. This was surprising for two reasons—behind my back they had nicknamed me "the bear" (partially deserved), and most had little or no extra money to spend on a nice gift like this.

It should have the director's name on it above mine.

FURTHER RESOURCES

Teachers exiting the profession have cited lack of support during the early years as a major contributor. Implementing mentoring programs and sustaining a culture where teachers feel free to ask for help are critical pathways to strengthen relationships within the school community so teachers feel supported.

For educators looking to learn more about how to shift mindsets around asking for help, *Reinforcements: How to Get People to Help You* by Heidi

Grant is a resource offering a framework and concrete steps for implementing. *Daring Greatly: How the Courage to be Vulnerable Transforms the Way we Live, Love, Parent, and Lead* by research professor and licensed social worker Brené Brown debunks the major myths around vulnerability so readers can understand the strength and power inherent to vulnerability.

Sociologist Wayne Baker's book *All You Have to Do Is Ask* provides an evidence base and blueprint for why we don't ask for the resources we need and how we can tap into the inherent generosity of those around us to help us achieve success. Finally, *Success is Possible: Creating a Mentoring Program to Support K-12 Teachers* by Stefanie R. Sorbet and Patricia Kohler-Evans lays out a foundation for teacher retention through mentorship.

Part V

PEDAGOGY AND INSTRUCTIONAL DECISIONS

Chapter 18

Missteps in Middle School English

Moving beyond Classroom Management and Content Mastery

Troy Hicks, PhD
Professor of English and Education
Central Michigan University

Fully convinced that I was in the right, I stomped over to the two offending students, snatched away their papers, and began to tear them into pieces. Before doing this, of course, I had warned everyone that they needed to stop talking since we were in the middle of a quiz.

Yet, these two were still at it.

It was early in the school year, during what was to become a weekly vocabulary quiz, and I needed to firmly establish control and precedent. As a young teacher, I knew that I needed to do something, anything to show students that I was serious.

Culprit number one, my chronic misbehavior, was Angelica. Unwilling to play by the rules or, at the very least, aiming to bend every single one of them, she was the one who not only chewed gum, but popped it. The one who forgot her pencil and, when you let her "borrow" one, made a show of sharpening it. Angelica. Very good at figuring out my pet peeves, pushing every button, and deflecting blame to her classmates.

She was sitting behind Rose who, for the most part, was an attentive, engaged, and amenable student. Not a likely suspect, but she was talking. Also, if I had been thinking about it, Rose was the one who brought her books to class, wrote in her journal when prompted, and was willing to raise her hand when I asked questions.

Eventually, I would come to understand that students like Rose generally did want to do well in school with the structures that were in place, including expectations for homework and tests, rules and routines. I would also come to learn later that Rose, in that moment before I grabbed her quiz away had, in her efforts to get Angelica to stop talking, simply turned around and told her to be quiet.

However, I wouldn't know, couldn't know in the moment, in the second week of my second year of teaching, because my teacher radar was not that finely attuned. So, there I was, standing in front of a room of about 25 eighth-graders in a rural middle school, struggling to know exactly what to do to establish some authority. Thus, I began ripping up two quizzes, setting an example to all who might choose to disobey.

Angelica, who was never going to be on my side anyway, simply smirked and shrugged her shoulders.

Rose, clearly horrified, would be the one that turned her allegiances against me for the rest of the year. In retrospect, this was a reasonable response.

The rest of the class, mouths slightly agape and eyes widened, quickly quieted down.

But, the quiet lasted only for that particular quiz, during that one particular hour. I am sure that students talked during the quiz I gave in the next hour, too, though—still trying to fully process what I had done—I didn't notice, nor did I rip up any more quizzes. I was quite shocked at my own behavior.

In that moment, I began to question everything that I knew about how to establish routines in my classroom, how to build relationships, and what I believed the role of assessment to be. Lessons about the first days of school and establishing rules, all from well-intentioned instructors in my teacher education methods courses, slipped away.

Having been an all A student myself, I began to wonder what all the tests and quizzes that I had aced from kindergarten forward ever really amounted to. In short, my fundamental understandings of "good" classroom manage-ment and high-quality assessment were both thrown into conflict that day, a misstep that has charted a path for every course, every workshop, and every webinar I have taught since then.

The memories of this one time when I tried to "establish authority" con-tinue to follow me in the undergraduate and graduate courses that I teach, as well as the professional development workshops that I lead. As a teacher educator who collaborates with and observes teachers in action, I recognize my own limitations (knowing that I do not regularly work with 75, 100, or 125 students over a span of 180 days, understanding their wants and needs in that intimate, challenging context).

Nor, knowing what researchers and educators know now about issues related to the persistent effects of poverty, institutional racism, and deep-seated trauma, can I say that I would be ready to do so.

Still, the core lesson from my teaching mistake holds true: I learned that I should never try to shame my students (or my colleagues) into compliance. I learned that I should never try to force them to demonstrate mastery through inauthentic assessments. And, I learned that I should not position myself in an overt display of authority, instead adopting the role of facilitator and coach.

While Rose was still a good student for the rest of the year, I know that my actions in that moment had soured any chance we might have at becoming truly connected. I had shattered a relationship. Also, as word spread that Mr. Hicks would "grab your paper and rip it up if you were talking," the initial shock and fear quickly wore off. Whatever I thought that I was doing to control my classes, it never really came to fruition.

I should have known better. I should have known better in the way that I had set up classroom routines, assessment protocols, and consequences for misbehavior, I failed to acknowledge many truths about human nature and basic educational psychology. I wish that I had known more about motivation, not to mention authentic assessment, at the time, and perhaps it wouldn't have made the mistake I did that day.

But, I did.

What I came to understand in my remaining years in the middle school classroom, through my subsequent work in graduate school, and now in over a decade of teacher education is that—regardless of their age, regardless of the content we are trying to teach, and regardless of what particular standards we are trying to reach—I set the conditions for learning, for better and for worse. What led me to the point of tearing up the quizzes that day cannot happen again, and here is how I avoid that situation all together.

It feels a bit overblown to say that this one moment, alone, helped redefine my priorities as an educator, yet here I am, laughing at my novice teaching self. That said, I know that some things are different than they were in the late 1990s.

First, there is no doubt that classroom management—including facets of building relationships, creating a community, and establishing norms and procedures—is still challenging for everyone, no matter what grade level or teaching context.

Second, there is also no doubt that assessment, whether mandated by the state or the district, and with a presumed or real pressure from parents or colleagues, is challenging, too. Recognizing these constraints, I still would argue that there are ways we can engage in more compassionate classroom management as well as authentic assessment practices.

Looking back on that moment where I confronted Rose and Angelica—taking their papers from them in an effort to establish control—I know I am still learning from my mistake. Like all good teachers, I know that I still have a great deal to learn, and I look to colleagues and mentors for continued guidance and support.

So, to Rose, I offer a long overdue apology and, to Angelica, I offer a more empathetic ear. My missteps became part of your seventh grade education. Were it possible to go back in time, I would make sure that I wasn't standing in front of the class preparing to rip up two quizzes (mostly because there wouldn't have been quizzes occurring that day). Instead, a more compassionate, authentic form of classroom management and assessment would have guided me. Though it's taken me quite some time, I still keep learning from my students, and I haven't given a vocabulary quiz in decades.

FURTHER RESOURCES

Catlin Tucker's ongoing discussions of blended learning in her high school English classroom are crucial, including recent posts like "Taking the 'Manage' Out of Classroom Management" (2018a) and "Blended Learning: 8 Respectful Routines" (2018b).

While there are so many voices that still seem to be dismissive of technology and the ways in which it can be used effectively, Tucker is one who is able to merge conversations about building relationships with students into an equally effective discussion about using technology for productive purposes.

For assessment, there are also a number of voices that resonate in contemporary conversations. Contributors that offer ideas on the website Teachers Going Gradeless provide real examples of authentic assessment.

Similarly, many voices that have gathered good ideas about writing appear in the collection *The Best Lesson Series: Writing: 15 Master Teachers Share What Works* (2018), edited by Brian Sztabnik, host of the *Talks with Teachers* podcast, who himself is also a voice of reason in current conversations about the teaching of English.

Finally, Gerard Dawson, another high school English teacher who, in recent months, has been prolific with blogging, offers us pieces on how to effectively teach peer feedback (2018a) and the aptly titled "Help Students Self-Assess Their Writing (Even If You're a Control Nut)" (2018b).

Chapter 19

The Power of the Mistake

Missteps and Instructional Decisions in Teaching Mathematics

Beth McCord Kobett, EdD
Associate Professor of Mathematics
Education, Stevenson University
Past President of the Association of Maryland
Mathematics Teacher Educators (AMMTE)
2000 Maryland Council of Teachers of Mathematics
(MCTM) Mathematics Educator of the Year

Every mistake I make teaching in the mathematics classroom is reflected back to me through my students' faces. I can see it the moment I make a mistake and it physically hurts me. Sometimes I can fix it in that instant, but most of the time I have to give myself space to figure out what happened and consider how I am going to heal all of us.

Of course, I am not talking about a calculation error or posting the wrong assignment. I am talking about mistakes that erode the *trust* I have worked so hard to build.

These mistakes include, but are not limited to, asking a student to share an idea when she wasn't ready to share because I wasn't paying enough attention to my students' verbal and physical cues, racing through a concept because, well, the test is coming up, or uttering the worst declarative statement ever, "This math concept is so easy!" followed by, "This math concept is going to be hard so let's buckle down."

Teachers can't take this teaching gig lightly. We can't assume that we don't have power in the classroom and that our teaching decisions don't have influence.

Our mistakes make a difference and have influence not just within the moment of the class, but in the students' future. These are mistakes that might change the trajectory of how students perceive themselves as mathematical thinkers and doers.

These mistakes may influence their beliefs about who they are and who they will become. For me, for example, in my present profession as a mathematics teacher educator, these mistakes may influence the way my students teach mathematics to others, which will, in turn, project beliefs about their students' competency and willingness to do mathematics. You see, this cycle is relentless. Therefore, we must always be vigilant.

One thing I do know, we, all of us, teach with the very best of intentions. Perhaps these aren't mistakes we make but rather missteps. Most of my own missteps are made out of concern for my students.

We desperately want our students to succeed, but sometimes the teaching slipups we make even when our hearts are in the right place have unintended consequences.

When this occurs, students exit the learning opportunity, whether it's one lesson, a full week of instruction, a unit of instruction, a course, or grade level with a belief that math should be understood immediately and without productive struggle, or incomplete understandings of mathematics concepts. And, if you don't know the answer quickly you are not likely going to get it.

The teaching moves that we make in *response* to mistakes can empower and engage students to develop an appreciation for and love of mathematics, which, in turn, will support them as they build positive beliefs about their ability to do mathematics. Teachers can learn a great deal from their students—as learning about how to be a good mathematics teacher is grounded in paying attention to how teaching decisions impact them.

First, let's begin with the premise that all children are brilliant. Most teachers are educated to find out what students don't know. This need to sniff out student deficiencies is a natural inclination fostered by years of first being a student and then later through an extensive preservice education background that focused on carefully and methodically seeking gaps to fix misunderstandings, and remedy faulty thinking.

The trouble with this mindset is that we are so focused on our students' deficits that we plow right past their strengths and the knowledge they bring to every learning encounter.

Many people grew up believing they were a "math person" or they weren't. Boiling a multidimensional subject like mathematics down to knowing some answers quickly, or in many cases, not knowing the answers, creates a one-dimensional view of mathematical competency. Such a view forces students to pick a side—I am good at this or I am not good at this. Early in my career, I found myself obsessed with documenting what students didn't know, creating an urgency in my classroom that alarmed my students, and quite frankly, myself.

The reality is that our students, and people in general, hold a variety of strengths described in *Adding It Up* as mathematical proficiencies (National Research Council, 2001).

Students can demonstrate proficiencies such as conceptual understanding in mathematics content focused on fractions, place value, geometry, and/or algebra; a productive disposition by demonstrating strengths like persistence; procedural fluency which is the ability to calculate efficiently and accurately; strategic competence, which is the ability to problem solve and represent solutions; adaptive reasoning, which is the ability justify, reflect, and explain ideas; and productive disposition which is seeing math as sensible, useful, and worthwhile.

All students hold strengths in one or more of these strands of mathematical proficiency and can use their strengths in a particular area to bolster their areas of challenge.

Instead of highlighting what students don't know, we can become strengths spotters to hone in on the mathematical brilliance of students. The strengths spotting should be applied to the student alone, not in comparison to another student or students. We tend to do a lot of comparing in education, and while that comparing can help find patterns that assist in anticipating and planning our instruction, it is typically not helpful to the individual.

Let's take a look at Samantha. Sam was a strong mathematical thinker, particularly when she could use and apply visual models to explain her ideas. She excelled when she could work with a partner to talk through her ideas and could typically find her own mistakes if she were given time to process. She was also very precise when using procedures. She frequently exhibited creative thinking using alternative solution pathways. She was challenged, however, when expected to produce an answer quickly.

When Sam arrived in my classroom, she told me, "I am not good at math." Her mother reported to me that she had heard the same exact sentence. I was baffled by this declaration but understood that Sam's understanding of her mathematical competency rested on her one mathematical challenge. Sam frequently found solution pathways that were novel, and, in fact, quite lovely.

Slowly, but surely, we began celebrating her strengths by naming them. We then used those strengths to build a bridge to procedural fluency competencies. Her need to fully understand mathematics and create solutions that made sense to her were strengths she shared with practicing mathematicians.

With the goal of making mathematics accessible, we often break mathematics down into parts and deliver small pieces of content to our students. Parsing mathematics into bite-sized chunks may work in the short term because students can produce answers, but when we do this, our students don't see how a small piece of mathematics that they are learning at a particular moment is connected to a more comprehensive set of conceptual ideas.

Any one of us who has uttered "But they knew it last week!" recognizes that students who learn small bits of information don't always see how they are connected. For example, a student I once interviewed, when asked to place 100 on a number line between 0 and 1000 placed it exactly between.

Despite my best efforts to ask just the right question that would help him self-correct, Michael vehemently defended his placement of 100.

Me: How many numbers are between 0 and 100?
Michael: 100.
Me: How many numbers are between 100 and 1000?
Michael: 900.
Me: (Waiting patiently for Michael to notice.)
Me: Where would 50 go?
Michael: Right in the middle between 0 and 100.
Me: Where would 500 go?
Michael: Right in the middle between 100 and 1000.
Me: (Still waiting patiently for Michael to notice his reasoning. After all, I taught him these units!)
Michael: [Sigh—breaking the silence] You see there is a pattern. He points at 0, one zero, points at 100, two zeros, and points at 1000, three zeros. We learned all about numbers to 100 and then we learned all about numbers from 100 to 1000. Don't ya see it?

Michael's thinking is quite interesting because he recognized a pattern by using his experiences learning about numbers and applied this segmented approach to learning about place value to this new situation. Yep, I knew it. Michael's understanding about the value and relationship of numbers was on me!

Instead of breaking down ideas, we should select rich mathematics tasks that encompass bigger ideas, which, in turn, provide more entry points for students to access the mathematics, develop mathematical language, and connect to prior learning and funds of knowledge. One way we can avoid this "bite-sized" trap is to present a meaty problem to students, facilitate student learning by asking probing questions, and then use the student work to unpack the mathematics in a meaningful, connected, and visible way.

For example, a teacher who wants to teach multiplication of fractions may present a problem like the following:

After the school picnic, you noticed that ¾ of the pan of brownies were left over. The principal asked you if she could take ⅓ of the pan of brownies to the school secretary to eat later. You get to take what is left home. How much of the full pan of brownies do you get to take home?

Instead of teaching the algorithm for multiplication of fractions first, students solve the problem by constructing representations and engaging in a productive discussion about the problem. Next, we use student solutions to make the mathematics visible and connect their representations to the procedures for multiplying fractions.

Students will then know why and how procedures work and are more likely to understand and remember the mathematics with meaning. When we do this, students feel like mathematically competent problem solvers and we share mathematical authority with them.

Early in my career, I was accused of planning too much—so much so that I began hiding my planning efforts lest I be teased by more experienced educators. Tired of the teasing and relentless cycle of planning, I tried to "wing" it and promptly fell flat on my face.

During this phase, one of my fifth graders asked, "Do you have any idea what we are doing?" It was then I knew I needed to trust myself. Planning made me feel more competent and less rushed. Thirty-five years later, this is still true.

Even for those of us that have taught for many years, taking the time to plan lessons alone or in collaborative teams makes a big difference in student learning. When I plan, I can select the most appropriate activity for my learners by considering their unique learning strengths and challenges. I can also anticipate how students will respond to the task or activity I have selected and map out different instructional paths they might take depending on the students' responses.

I also regularly anticipate how to use formative assessment techniques throughout the lesson and can prepare to respond in ways that promote student understanding. I can pose thoughtful questions that probe students to try another strategy or justify their thinking.

Without such focused, learner-centered planning, I may fall into a "corrective feedback" loop in which I prompt students to give and get answers without understanding. This thoughtful planning allows me to be present in the lesson. Presence in a lesson is that moment when it almost feels like time stops or at least slows—there is a kind of symbiotic energy that is created in our classroom community as students recognize that I am truly listening to hear their mathematical thinking, strategies, and solution pathways.

When I am lucky, and things go as planned, these moments become generative as students clamor to share their ideas in this very special space we have created. I know that I won't have a chance at these moments unless I have thoroughly, thoughtfully, and purposefully targeted my planning for my students.

We make so many instructional decisions! Every decision I make sets off a ripple within the classroom. How I decide how to group my students, what tasks I share, what materials to use in a lesson, questions I will pose, and so much more. Grouping students by perceived ability sends clear messages to students about their capability to do mathematics.

During my third year of teaching, my students were grouped by mixed ability by edict from the district's curriculum office. What first frightened me because I didn't know how I could meet all my students' needs ended up enlightening me to the power of heterogeneous classes. I quickly learned that by varying my grouping to promote students' strengths and interests fostered collaboration skills and built positive student dispositions about learning mathematics.

This new grouping practice forced me to construct tasks that were relevant to them (e.g., Pokemon and skateboarding!) and invited different perspectives and competencies.

Making mistakes is part of every teacher's growth. The power of the mistake resides in paying attention to how my instructional decisions impact my students. The power to go beyond such missteps comes from knowing that students who have their ideas recognized and valued can develop positive beliefs about themselves as capable and empowered mathematical learners.

Chapter 20

Beyond Finding and Fixing Error

Responding to Student Work

Sara Heaser
Lecturer of English at the University of Wisconsin La Crosse

I teach four sections of first-year writing per semester at the university level. My students write a lot, which means I read student writing a lot. It's rewarding and exciting work, but there's just so *much* of it. It's a fragile balance between being efficient and being engaging. It's a victory if I can accomplish both.

Early in my teaching career, when the uncertainty of the unknown drove me to overcompensate in meticulously planned classroom activities and dense syllabi, I was desperate for an antidote to the crushing workload I had not yet learned to manage. When I found an app that streamlined the feedback process, I was hooked.

Instead of reading printed versions of student papers and commenting on them in the margins by hand (a time-consuming and mentally exhausting endeavor), I could read them on my tablet, check a few boxes, and select from a variety of pre-written comments to include as "my" feedback.

If an essay felt disorganized, for example, I chose the "structure" category and scrolled through sentences that noted paragraphing, focus, connecting ideas, or whatever keyword best matched the issue at hand. Once completely finished, these sentences were automatically formatted into a quasi-letter for the student to read. I avoided accountability further by choosing a letter grade the "feedback" seemed to best reflect.

A few days after I had returned essays using this app for the first time, a student came to my office. He didn't know why he received the grade he did, and he wanted an explanation. Immediately. He sneered, "You said my writing was like a car stuck in the mud. That the wheels turn but it's not really going anywhere." He emphasized "you." *YOU said.*

I blubbered my way through this prickly confrontation by restating points in the letter I had "written." It was cryptic and directive. Change this, move that, develop that. The student sat, mostly silent. Our conversation was, well, no more than wheels spinning in mud. As he started to pack his bag, much remained unresolved between us.

The student had laid bare himself on the page and out of self-interest, I had reduced his efforts to an off-handed, insensitive analogy that I did not remember clicking on in the first place. Any wisp of trust he had in me, any enthusiasm he might've had for writing, evaporated as soon as he read that comment, and our meeting did nothing to help.

I didn't get it. I was giving and giving feedback, but hardly any students mentioned or even acknowledged it. The switch to this app seemed like a solution. If they weren't reading my feedback or doing anything with it, what was the point? I could keep giving students what I was supposed to be giving them, only much faster. Why then, did it feel like I was spinning my wheels in mud? When that student left my office though, I finally acknowledged and questioned the resistance I was sensing.

To move from novice to reflective practitioner requires a mental shift just like this: a shift to a purposeful, metacognitive sense of self-awareness within a larger educational context. Novice teachers may approach pedagogy internally and inadvertently design curriculum with themselves at the center: their knowledge, their goals, their classroom spaces, and in my case, their meticulously planned classroom activities and dense syllabi.

Naturally, our awareness of our power and influence is limited at first; we instead focus on what we can physically control, like the cadence of a lecture or the exact due date of an assignment. And that makes sense; we're nervous and figuring it out.

But instead, consider a teacher's presence from the outside in; look first at where your influence lingers external to the classroom. The margins of an essay happen to be just one of the many spaces where students listen to our ideas. We are always reinforcing what we value when we give feedback, wherever it is given. And students are always listening, far beyond the classroom.

So, it's important to ask those classic investigative questions that lead us into metacognition: the who, what, where, why, and how of our feedback practices. For example, how do you provide feedback in your course? And, why this way? The most dynamic, effective teachers continuously interrogate their own practices, change something, fail a little, talk with others about this failure, try again, and in the end, get better.

When confiding with a mentor about the app disaster, with some gentle interrogation (which is what the best mentors do), I got it. As a new teacher, assessment and feedback still meant the same thing to me. I had yet to realize that responding to and assessing learning are two entirely different actions inspired by entirely different intentions. I thought I was providing feedback on student writing, but I was instead assessing it.

Assessment often stems from places beyond the classroom: in committees, departments, districts, and even within entire states. It can focus on things like outcomes, benchmarks, gains, criteria, and many other official-sounding words.

Assessment and the design, execution, and evaluation of it is important. In the broadest sense of the term, it helps us know whether learning is happening, whether students have met a particular learning goal. Students learn in environments shaped by assessment parameters, but that doesn't necessarily mean they're aware of these parameters and how they may impact their experiences. And of course, what to assess, and how, among many other contextual factors, can be contentious among parties involved.

On the other hand, feedback is less about deciding whether a student has met a goal and more about having a conversation *with* a learner *about* reaching a goal *together*. To give feedback is to *respond*—to begin a conversation that can encourage learners to engage in a process of inquiry. So, back to wheels in mud. Is that comment feedback or assessment?

It sounds and feels like feedback, but it is not. It did not invite conversation. The student did not know what my comment meant. He did not know why I said it. And he certainly did not know what to do with it. Similarly, feedback is not a grade on a report card, a big red number or a sticker at the top of a page, or even surface-level edits in red ink. There is no conversation here, no exchange of ideas between novice and mentor.

How to create this conversation, then? What follows are two key strategies that value quality over quantity. First, give early-intervention feedback. Provide feedback to students as they engage in their work, not *after* they've completed it.

Assign, collect, and respond to things like research questions, quizzes, bibliographies, topic ideas, thesis statements, outlines or mock-ups, and such. Respond does not mean writing "9/10. Good job!" at the top of a worksheet. That's assessment. Write a complete sentence that doesn't sound like a to-do list. Hypothesize. Ponder. Wonder. Ask a question that provokes a thought and a response.

Early-intervention feedback should be consistently everywhere, all the time. Give students feedback before, after, and during class or in the hallways. Give feedback to the entire class by noting patterns you see and bringing attention to them; give feedback in small group conferences; have students give each other feedback. Give feedback on post-it notes, verbally, in emails, on a Screencast—anywhere. Start looking at all the interactive spaces that already exist, from the outside in.

By engaging in early-intervention feedback, teachers can become familiar with the student's intentions, processes, and struggles; there's more investment in the *process* of learning, rather than the product. I had none of this rich context when firing off pre-written statements on that poor student's essay. That student and I, we both missed out on an incredible opportunity to learn from each other, which guts me still now, years later.

Along with early-intervention feedback, purposely invite students to be the first and primary voice in the feedback process with reflection. This metacognitive practice mentioned earlier has been tied closely to student learning gains in many studies. Feedback, utilized as a reflective catalyst, can empower students with a sense of agency in their learning spaces.

Have students submit a piece of reflection alongside their work. It could be a letter to you, highlighting the key things they learned and yet struggled with; it could be a list of questions they have for you and to which they would like you to respond; it could be including a few key pieces from their process alongside the final project; it could even be a daily "exit ticket" that touches on three points: what they now know; what they want to know; what they still don't understand.

What did I know about that student's intentions for his piece? The choices he made while drafting? His worries or concerns about his draft? Not a thing. Get the context.

Again and again, reading student reflections alongside their work, I'm nodding my head in agreement, excited to continue the conversation they started. Much of the time, students have a more accurate sense of themselves as learners than they realize; their reflections tell me more about what they understand than the product they've produced does; and that in some ways, teachers are less important than we think we are. We can carefully set the stage for learning, but we certainly don't need to run the show.

When first adopting these practices, guilt may settle in: Are students getting enough feedback? Feedback might feel ephemeral, tough to pin down—it might not be in a rubric or gradebook or another official, organized place. It might be hard to let go of the false sense of security that points, checks, and record-keeping offer. You might have to learn to trust yourself, and more importantly, students.

Dispersing feedback far and wide requires careful course planning; you'll need to scaffold carefully to position feedback as recursive steps, necessary to a unit or project instead of tagging it on as a last, single to-do item. Doing this requires looking far beyond the day-to-day lesson planning and into effective course design. Again, starting from the outside in—looking beyond yourself first, or, what pedagogical scholars call "backward design."

Lastly, a larger challenge. This approach to feedback, built locally and organically from the bottom up, also directly contradicts how assessment is often imposed, which is from the top down.

As teachers, we all know that our classrooms do not function in isolation—our day-to-day work is closely watched by others who may carry agendas that differ from our own. There's no escaping pressure for students to perform well on more traditional assessment measures like standardized exams, which, ideologically, seem at ends with intentionally informal, early-intervention feedback. Where is the balance?

The very first step is to recognize how your own teaching practice may fit into larger institutional contexts and how you might find spaces for authentic conversation with your students in spite of constraints.

FURTHER RESOURCES

A few key resources that helped me shift ideologically and practically to understanding the importance of effective feedback were Nancy Sommer's slim, accessible, and affordable text *Responding to Student Writers* and

Ed White's perennial book, *Assigning, Responding, Evaluating: A Writing Teacher's Guide.*

Sommer's volume focuses on responding to student writers as holistic learners, not necessarily to errors or mistakes found in writing. White also unpacks the purposes of feedback, which you can see demonstrated in the title, as he positions "Responding" and "Evaluating" as two separate verbs.

Finally, Carol Dweck's research on mindset and her bestseller *Mindset: The New Psychology of Success* inspired me to pay careful attention to how I interact and converse with my students so they can understand learning as a process of trial and error.

Chapter 21

Lesson Plans Would Be So Easy
If It Weren't for the Students

Debbie Silver, EdD

In interviews I'm often asked to talk about any fundamental mistakes I made as a classroom teacher. My customary response is, "How much time do you have?" Like most reflective teachers, I look back on what are now obvious missteps in my teaching journey and wonder how my students and I survived.

In my defense, I began my teaching career as a 20-year-old college sophomore with zero hours in education and absolutely no training as a teacher. What was supposed to be a year as a "temporary substitute" turned into a 30-year career. We will leave that story for another time.

I began my career as a first-grade teacher but eventually found my way to my preferred assignment—middle-school science teacher. With virtually no experience in science or in middle-level learning I was wedded to my teacher's manual for lesson planning. I aligned my manual's table of contents with the school calendar (early example of a pacing guide) so that I could be sure I covered each chapter by the end of the year.

I spent hours creating specific plans for each science unit. I diligently sought out engaging activities, ordered films to show, prepared worksheets for the students, planned my lecture presentations complete with class notes for the students, and wrote questions for classroom discussions and end of chapter tests. I organized, designed, and practiced so that I could teach my "perfect lessons." (I've sometimes been accused of being a bit OCD, but we're not going there right now.)

Confident that I was ready to cover each new chapter, I would introduce the topic with a typical rhetorical question such as: "So do you remember from last year about how the systems of the human body work?" I smiled and bobbed my head to cue a "yes" answer so I could get right to my flawlessly designed lesson plan. I barely gave my students time to mumble their "uh-huh's," and away I'd go. I had much to cover and precious little time to do it.

It wasn't that I didn't realize some students might not be up to speed quite yet on the topic of the day or that others might have already mastered things I was presenting as new knowledge. I just felt I could help the strugglers catch up as we went along, and I could direct the high-flyers to the *Going Further* resource section at the end of the chapter.

I now regret how my "full steam ahead" approach to lesson delivery missed one of the most essential elements in good teaching—*pre-assessment*. Or to put it another way—finding out ahead of time what the heck each and every one of my students knew or did not know about a particular topic.

I presented my lessons with no clue about their prior knowledge, skill levels, or level of interest. My lessons were well-intentioned and full of energy, but they were never as successful as they could have been.

I thought I was differentiating instruction because I often used cooperative learning, varied my instructional techniques, and occasionally threw in an alternative assessment. But I missed that one critical reality. It is impossible to differentiate instruction effectively (in other words, reach each student where they are) without using purposeful pre-assessment.

I had heard the term "pre-assessment" thrown around in teacher workshops, but I didn't think I had time to spend on a pretest or even to employ simple strategies like doing a K-W-L chart or a Gallery Walk to assess what students knew. I had so much I wanted to tell and show them, and I needed to get right to it.

I don't know how the importance of pre-assessment eluded me for so long. One would never go back to a doctor who made a diagnosis or prescribed a round of medicine without a thorough examination that included a review of one's medical history, right?

And how much tolerance do we teachers have for mandated professional development that merely repeats information we already know? When it finally sunk in, I knew I had to at least try some pre-assessment strategies.

Through trial and error, I finally learned how much more effective I could be by slowing down long enough to figure out exactly where my learners were *before* I prepared my meticulous "perfect lessons." Once I made the time to pre-assess their learning as a first step, I realized that I actually saved time in the long run. And once I let my lessons follow a more natural ebb and flow, both the students and I were happier.

Often, I found that students were far more informed than I had previously thought and just needed some prompts to remind them of what they already knew. I would say, "With a partner take this outline of the human body and draw me what you know about its major systems. You can use pictures, words, and phrases. This is to let me know what you already know and will not be graded." I would move around the room listening for comprehension, factual integrity, and other information I needed to proceed with my plans.

Other times, I realized I had overestimated my students' understanding of a topic. Some of them strongly held naïve ideas that needed to be addressed. One pair of students wrote, "Every system has its own set of organs that work only for that system." (Uh-oh, I needed to "unteach" that concept.)

Ultimately, I learned to invest the extra time up front and find out more about each of my 6 sections of 30 different learners. In the end, it greatly streamlined the teaching–learning process for all of us. (Hang on—I've got some ideas to share about how to do this.)

I finally realized there was no way I could help students reach that optimal learning place between challenge and accomplishment without predetermining from where they were starting. I could no longer just walk in and start "teaching" to the students I assumed they were.

Instead of being irritated by the high-flyer kid who took one look at my lab setup and said, "Oh I know what we're doing today. I've done this before, and I already know what's going to happen," I learned to respond, "After looking at the pre-assessment, I had a feeling you might be ahead of the rest of the class on this concept. Here's an activity I found I think will challenge you and give you a chance to learn something new, too."

Rather than merely being sympathetic to strugglers who lagged, I realized I needed to modify my instructional strategies ahead of time to provide them opportunities to learn new material within their current reach. Consistently presenting them with expectations far beyond their grasp only reinforced their feelings of helplessness and futility. Ironically, when I focused more on their incremental gains and less on end-of-the-chapter test scores, both their interest and their grades increased.

It's hard for students and their teachers to know how far they've progressed without an accurate assessment of where they began. A nongraded evaluation is imperative. Consider:

- Prescribed pre-tests can provide documentation of where students started.
- Comparing their pretest results to their summative assessments yields far more valuable information to the students, their parents, and the teacher than any standardized or departmental test.
- Focusing on growth rather than on finite scores inspires incremental (growth) mindsets and helps to build self-efficacy in learners.
- *Informal* pre-assessments can be woven into discussions, introductory activities, and engaging undertakings.

I figured out how to use all manner of strategies to identify experiential backgrounds, individual interests, prior knowledge while uncovering misconceptions students had about different topics. Thankfully, ideas for pre-assessment abound on the internet (and there's always Pinterest for the "creativity-challenged" teacher like me).

KWL Charts: K-what does the student know? W-what does the student need and want to know? L-what did the students learn? The "K" and the "W" are effective pre-assessment tools. The "L" can be used as part of a summative evaluation allowing students to share the depth of knowledge they gained in the unit of study. K-W-L templates are readily available on the internet.

Number Line: Large numerals from 1 to 8 are mounted on a classroom wall or in the hall. With 8 being strong agreement, and 1 being strong disagreement, students stand under the number that best represents their current state in regard to teacher-posed statements such as, "I understand how the human body systems work well enough to teach someone else." You can even snap a picture of where students stand to compare with the one you take when asking the same question at the end of the unit.

Yes/No/Kind of/Cards: Each student gets a set of three cards. Teachers ask a series of questions asking if students understand certain essential ideas in the upcoming unit. Students respond with either a "yes" or "no" card. If they are ambivalent, they hold up the "kind of" card. The cards can be different colors for easy identification, or they can be the same color with the words printed boldly enough for the teacher (but not others) to see.

Gallery Walk: The teacher identifies what knowledge or skills to assess and writes a different question and/or prompt at the top of posters placed around classroom walls. Each student or student group receives a different colored marker so later the teacher is able to identify which responses belong to which learner(s). The teacher keeps the time and has students rotate through the posters at specific intervals to respond to questions or make comments. Later the teacher reviews student answers to examine where students are in their learning and plans next steps in instruction.

Graffiti Wall: With colorful markers and large poster or unrolled paper, students creatively design a graffiti wall of things they know about a specific topic of study. The teacher stands to the side asking probing questions and making notes about things that do or do not need to go into plans for the unit. Teachers can leave the wall up and encourage students to add to it throughout the unit as they gain new knowledge.

Silent Brainstorming: Divide students into groups of four or five. Give each group a large piece of paper or poster. Give each group member a pad of sticky notes. With absolutely NO talking, everyone has three minutes to post as many ideas, explanations, bits of information, or questions as they can (each is written on a different sticky note) on the poster paper. After three minutes, group members discuss and organize their notes. They combine their ideas into two or three summarizing sentences and write them at the bottom. Each group then presents their sticky note-covered poster, with summary statements, to the entire class.

Of course, it was much easier to plan the "perfect lesson" when no actual students were around to mess things up, but we all know it doesn't work like that. The teaching–learning process is a constantly evolving practice that relies on assessing, planning, executing, monitoring, adjusting, and getting/giving feedback.

It takes time and requires flexibility. I no longer want to be locked into a fixed plan that does not allow me the freedom to teach the unplanned lesson that presents itself on a particular day. The best lessons I have taught are generally ones that included spontaneity and strayed far from my original plan because I taught students instead of a lesson plan.

Today I cannot imagine teaching a lesson without the valuable roadmap that pre-assessment provides. When I work with teachers who tell me, "I just don't have the time to do all this pre-assessment stuff," I respond, "You don't have the time not to. It will improve your teaching in ways you never imagined, and not doing it was one of the biggest teaching mistakes I ever made."

Chapter 22

The Limits of Teacher Preparation
Learning to Make Pedagogy Actionable

Pasi Sahlberg
Finnish educator and global thought leader, author, scholar

My first job was to be a math and science teacher in Helsinki in one of the middle and high schools over there, and it was my dream job really—that's what I wanted to do for the rest of my life. That was where I started.

The school where I was teaching was part of the University of Helsinki, part of their teacher training establishment there. I moved to the Department of Teacher Education, which was practically part of the school, and so I kept my connection to the school, but I was also teaching the new teachers in math and science. Then I moved on to look at that school and other schools from the systems perspective as a curriculum expert at the National Agency for Education.

I felt prepared when I entered the classroom in terms of the content. I was teaching mathematics, physics, and chemistry, and I felt I was very prepared to teach from the point of view of the subject matters.

I probably felt a little bit less prepared to plan my classes and in terms of knowing how to teach, but I think the initial teacher education really prepared me not as much in terms of the depth of pedagogy, but provided a wide range of ideas.

When I graduated and left to teach, I felt I had a great amount of ideas for what to do, and much less knowledge of how to do these things. That is where I felt unprepared. At that time, I felt, as did many of my colleagues, this is where the practice and experience comes into the picture.

We felt that we would learn while we were in practice and we would just try things out.

Overall I felt I was prepared to do what I needed to in the classroom. I was much less prepared to do what I was supposed to do in the staff room with my much more experienced colleagues. That's where the teacher education in Finland was much weaker and I think still is. I believe that young people who go to teach, like myself, are much less ready to understand the culture of the school and what happens among the teachers in the school.

That's something that is very well understood right now in the current conversations in Finland when it comes to teacher education—how important it is to understand the culture of the professionals, teachers, leadership, and others in addition to what's happening in your classroom. I think I was much more prepared to do things when I was in the classroom and much less prepared to understand what my role was or what I was supposed to do and what I could do with my colleagues in the staffroom.

The one big difference between the practice in the United States and Finland is that in my country teachers, young and old, have much more time and opportunity to interact and spend time with their colleagues. I've been in many schools, particularly in New York City, where there is no physical space where teachers could get together, cooperate, work together, and have a conversation.

In Finland, if you go to any school, anywhere, there's always a teachers lounge and there's a space for teachers to sit down and have a conversation. In addition, Finnish teachers have much less required instruction every day than in the United States. So I think it's not so much that question of what teachers should do, but what the day of a teacher should look like so that they could really understand the importance of teaching being a collective cooperative profession rather than an individual thing.

I think a difference between the American culture of teaching and the Finnish one is that in Finland, probably everywhere, it's thought of as a collective effort to help young people learn and grow and be educated. Whereas in the United States, in my experience and what I've heard from colleagues and friends, this is seen as a much more individual thing, and teachers in America are held *individually* accountable for doing what they do. This is a huge issue when it comes to how to prepare new teachers to understand what the teaching profession is all about.

Social media and technology and the opportunities they bring to connect with teachers and others in the profession is helpful, but it can never do what the face-to-face interaction, the sense of being in the same space, and really understanding the emotions and feelings, the experience of others, can do.

If someone believes we can use technology and the devices it provides to connect teachers and do the same thing you can do when you sit down to have a cup of coffee, a pint of beer, or sitting around the table and trying to understand what others are doing—that will never happen in the online space.

This has always been my advice to the policymakers in the United States: if you really want to make teaching an attractive and a true profession, the only way to do that is to make sure all teachers, everybody, has space—a physical space—and a license to take a good part of the day to spend together and have a conversation face to face.

This is not just Finland that implements this. Look at Japan, a country that America admires a lot as a model for education—what the Japanese, or Singaporean, or Chinese, or Koreans do.

They have a lot of time for teachers during the school day to sit down and observe and talk about one another's lessons and observe them and plan together. American teachers very rarely have this privilege of having face-to-face conversations and interactions. I think the technology, be it social media or digital gadgets, can provide some things, but it can never do the same thing as the real, physical interaction can do. And this is what teachers know very well.

I want to really emphasize the importance of giving teachers time during the school day to really work like a professional.

Think about what the other professionals do every day on the job—what their working day looks like in the law firm, or hospital, or architect design studio, for example. What do people do with their time every day? A big part of the day for a medical doctor or a surgeon, for example, is to sit down with their colleagues and figure out what to do with this case, what to do with this patient.

It is not totally about performing the operation but also about thinking *with others* about how to do this operation. Or when lawyers work, their work is not just in the courthouse and representing the client—a big part of their time is spent sitting with their colleagues and thinking about how to do that work.

But if you look at teachers, particularly in the United States, but also in many other countries, most of the time they teach alone without support or help from anyone else.

That's the kind of thing—in America, if you really want to elevate the teaching profession, educators need to have time to build this culture of conversation and professional collaboration. To talk about what they do and try to understand not only what I do as a teacher, but also what my colleagues are doing and how they do their work. This is exactly what the high-performing countries like Japan, Korea, Singapore, China, Finland, or Canada are doing. The teachers have time to talk about what they do, and by talking about what they do, they better understand what they should do in the classroom, and that's what's missing in America.

FURTHER RESOURCES

The New Zealand Ministry of Education hosts a useful tool for analyzing one's school culture at https://www.educationalleaders.govt.nz/Culture/Understanding-school-cultures/What-is-our-school-culture-like.

The checklist teachers can download there includes audits on teaching and learning issues, teacher strategy and planning culture, staff issues, resourcing, the local community, and general culture issues. Once teachers can see the issues within and across school culture that impact how they carry out their work with students and with each other, they can feel more empowered in their careers and lives.

Sahlberg, P., & Walker, T. (2021). *In Teachers We Trust: The Finnish Way to World-Class Schools*. New York: W. W. Norton.

Discussion Questions

PART I: DIVERSITY, EQUITY, AND INCLUSION

1. How can educators become aware of gaps in their knowledge of the cultures of and within the schools in which they teach?
2. Baldwin points out that cultural features in a community are not necessarily visible on websites or in statistical reporting. How can teachers identify and better understand (and ultimately accommodate) these features?
3. In what ways have you encountered ableism in or out of educational contexts?
4. Have you ever felt limited or excluded by the classroom environment—what specifically made you feel this way?
5. How might school curricula in your content area perpetuate ableism?
6. How can teachers learn about the economic conditions in which their students live to teach with more sensitivity and relevance?
7. What advice would you give to teachers about the language they use both in the classroom and in their individual work with students? Does this advice extend to the words of others (such as authors of published books and articles)?

PART II: REFRAMING ASSUMPTIONS

1. In what respects are you a gatekeeper in your classroom? What high stakes decisions do you make and what power do you consciously or unconsciously wield?

2. Have there been times you might have underestimated a student or colleague? What happened that made you realize you had judged wrongly?

3. How can we design experiences beyond the classroom that give students the chance to reveal their abilities and identities in their full complexity?

4. How can we design learning experiences that give students more of a voice—and help us learn what gifts each person might bring to the task?

5. What cultural norms or social underpinnings have shaped you personally or as an educator?

6. Where has bias or ethnocentricity made its way into your classroom or teaching practice?

PART III: FOSTERING RELATIONSHIPS AND ADVOCATING FOR STUDENTS

1. Jarzabek suggests that a teacher should "know their stuff " in order to be an advocate. How might knowing yourself including your own biases be an important part of this knowledge?

2. What skills should you further develop to enable you to better develop your "teacher voice?"

3. What can you do when advocating for your students does not bring the desired results?

4. Why is it important that teachers reflect on and alter their teaching practice?

5. What are some specific actions teachers can take to ensure students can safely develop their voices within the realm of school?

6. What are some practical ways that students can take action or make their ideas public, both inside and beyond the walls of school?

7. How do you honor yourself and your learners within your classroom space?

8. Why is integrating student thinking and student voice into planning and instruction important? How are you currently doing this and how do you want to grow?

9. What communication and conflict resolution skills are most important for teachers to develop?

10. Describe the most difficult class you've had in regard to student buy-in. What was difficult about it? Were students rowdy/rambunctious, or

overly quiet? What techniques did you use to overcome these hurdles, and how did it shape your teaching moving forward?

PART IV: CREATING RESPONSIVE ENVIRONMENTS FOR STUDENT LEARNING

1. When you think about the texts or topics you teach, how do they connect to the lived experiences of your students? Will this be something they are very familiar with and is this something that they probably have very little experience with? Is this something they may have strong positive or negative feelings toward? Is this something that could make class discussions uncomfortable? If so, why?

2. Trust is central to student learning in that students need to trust their teachers have subject matter expertise and that they care about their well-being to be willing to engage. What do students need to help them engage within your content area? If you don't know the answer to this question, who in your community can help you find solutions?

3. What kind of anxieties do students bring into the classroom and how teachers mitigate these anxieties so they can better access opportunities for learning?

4. What are some methods teachers can use to connect with students as individuals rather than as members of a class of students?

5. Where do you engage binary thinking in your teaching and how can you work to broaden your perspective to better connect with students?

6. What forces cause teachers to be reticent to ask for help?

7. What human resources do teachers have available when they need help and how can institutions improve their access to these resources?

PART V: PEDAGOGY AND INSTRUCTIONAL DECISIONS

1. Reading about mistakes does not allow us to infer how and why these mistakes (or their avoidance) might lead to excellence in teaching, especially as it relates to instructional decisions and actions. How can educators recognize when something isn't working and learn from mistakes and failure to move toward more effective classroom practices?

2. Has there been a time where you caught a student cheating (or, thought that you caught a student cheating)? How did you manage it in the moment? As a follow-up to the event?

3. How did you learn to provide feedback to students? What were your own experiences receiving feedback like as a student?

4. Where and how do you see evidence that your students are engaging with your feedback? What does this evidence say about what they're learning? About how they're learning? About your own role in the classroom?

5. How does not only learning from your failure but also owning it with your students help model how to take a failure and make it a positive or mitigate its damage?

6. Are the stories in this volume idiosyncratic or universally applicable? How can episodic failure be fruitfully integrated into a broader career path as an educator?

About the Editor

Julie Warner left the classroom fewer than 10 years ago—close enough that she can still vividly remember her first few rocky years with their emotional and logistical landmines, but long enough to have had a career in education since then that includes obtaining a doctorate in education from Teachers College, Columbia University, stints as an education policy advisor in the U.S. Senate and the White House, and overseeing the teacher issues portfolio within the U.S. Department of Education's internal think tank.

Even as she's advised on high-level policy decisions in education, she's always stayed close to the classroom: she's a National Board Certified Teacher and has published a book on teaching teens with smartphones (2016), coedited a book on teaching with technology (2019), published several recent articles on classroom teaching for professional journals for teachers, and is a journalist for Course Hero's Faculty Club, one of the top 250 sites on the web.

About the Contributors

Chris Anson, PhD, is distinguished university professor, professor of English, and director of the Campus Writing and Speaking Program at North Carolina State University.

Anna Baldwin spent 20 years as an English teacher on the Flathead Indian Reservation before moving into the district grants manager position and is the 2014 Montana Teacher of the Year.

Katherine Baker is an assistant professor in the Department of Education at Elon University and holds a doctorate in curriculum and instruction from the University of North Carolina at Chapel Hill.

Christopher Bass is a doctoral candidate at the University of Illinois Chicago. He taught English language arts and executive functioning skills for over a decade.

Andy Boyle is an instructional technology specialist at Kennesaw State University iTeach. Andy has over 10 years of teaching experience, most of them in economics classrooms.

Sarah Cheatle is a 14th year high school English teacher and PhD student focusing on transgender studies.

Mark DiMauro is a professor at the University of Pittsburgh and teaches digital humanities alongside composition and rhetoric.

Kate Haq has been a professional educator since 1985 and currently teaches at the Park School, an independent progressive school in Buffalo, New York.

Sara Heaser is a lecturer of English at the University of Wisconsin La Crosse, where she specializes in basic and first-year writing curriculum, pedagogy, and program development.

Troy Hicks, PhD, is professor of English and education at Central Michigan University (CMU) and director of the Chippewa River Writing Project.

Beth Jarzabek is an eighth-grade language arts teacher and holds a Master of Arts in teacher leadership from Mount Holyoke.

Beth McCord Kobett, EdD, is a professor in the School of Education at Stevenson University, and received the Mathematics Educator of the Year Award from the Maryland Council of Teachers of Mathematics.

Mike Land directs the Community Service-Learning Program at Assumption University where he utilizes CSL in journalism, creative writing, and literature courses.

Darius Phelps is a Pre-K Specialist with the Georgia Department of Early Care and Learning. He formerly taught at Dunwoody Elementary in DeKalb County Public Schools District. In 2015, he received a Bachelor of Science degree and in 2019 a Master of Education degree from the University of Georgia.

Lisa Power teaches marketing and leadership at Saint Martin's University in Lacey, Washington. She holds a PhD in leadership studies from Gonzaga University.

Jane Saunders, PhD, is an associate professor in reading/literacy education at Texas State University and holds a doctorate from the University of Texas at Austin.

Pasi Sahlberg has worked as teacher, teacher educator, researcher, and policy advisor in Finland. He is a professor of education policy at the University of New South Wales in Sydney, Australia.

Debbie Silver is an educator, speaker, author, and humorist. She has over 30 years of experience as a teacher, staff development specialist, and university professor.

Alaina Smith taught for five years and is now a program coordinator for the William H Thompson Scholars Learning Community at the University of Nebraska-Lincoln.

Kip Téllez is professor and former chair in the Education Department at UC Santa Cruz. His most recent book is titled *The Teaching Instinct*.

Peter Warner has a degree in business administration and computer science and taught computer programming at the college level.

Bobson Wong has taught math in New York City public high schools since 2005 and is a three-time recipient of the Math for America Master Teacher Fellowship and is a New York State Master Teacher.